HEART & $OUL OF MARKETING

ENDORSEMENTS

"Matt Romania's book is a vital resource for anyone looking to elevate their communication strategies.
This book is a concise, practical and experience-based guide for those committed to driving meaningful change through their work."

- Jimmy Wales, Founder, Wikipedia.org

"This book offers concise and clear planning resources, enhanced by Matt Romania's genuine voice and personal anecdotes. It stands out by making essential information both accessible and engaging."

- Jane Caro AM, Author

"If you want practical guidance on how to 'do' marketing to achieve results for your charity - greater awareness, stronger relationships with donors and more charitable funds, this is the guide for you. It provides a treasure trove of ideas and action guides that make this book a key for your charity's success."

- Katherine Raskob, CEO, Fundraising Institute Australia

"Matt Romania has delivered thoughtful and practical assistance for anyone involved in the competitive charity, philanthropic, sector. A must read for individuals and organisations wanting to amplify their positive impact."

- Kristin Stegley AM, National Trust of Victoria Foundation

HEART & SOUL OF MARKETING

MATT ROMANIA

Published by Brolga Publishing Pty Ltd
ABN 46 063 962 443
PO Box 452
Torquay Victoria 3228
Australia

email: markzocchi@brolgapublishing.com.au

National Library of Australia
Cataloguing-in-Publication data

Matt Romania, author. ISBN: 978-1-7636801-3-5 (paperback)

A catalogue record for this book is available from the National Library of Australia

Printed in Australia
Cover design and typeset by Alanna Rance, Little Nook Creative.

BE PUBLISHED
Publish through a successful publisher
National Distribution to Australia & New Zealand
International Distribution to the United Kingdom

This book is dedicated to my beautiful wife, Karina, the most creative and kind person. Also to Juliette, Lacey and Baby #3, may this serve as inspiration for you to achieve what you want in life, and a reminder to explore and find the causes and communities that resonate with you. May you continue to explore this world with curiosity, strength and hope.

CONTENTS

THE FIRST STORYTELLERS

The author acknowledges Aboriginal and Torres Strait Islander peoples as Traditional Custodians and the first storytellers of the lands on which we live and work. I honour Aboriginal and Torres Strait Islander peoples' connection to Country and celebrate Aboriginal and Torres Strait Islander stories, traditions and living cultures - and pay respects to Elders past and present.

PREFACE

Why This Book Exists

This book isn't about my personal journey; it's about you and your aspirations to create a positive impact on the world. Before diving into the framework, let me share with you why this book exists, as it almost didn't come to fruition. I had considered writing a book several times, but I didn't want to contribute yet another marketing book to the already saturated and noisy landscape that charity organisations face daily. Charities receive advice from all directions, often contradictory, sometimes intentionally misleading, and can result in generic recommendations that can damage brand reputation and waste valuable time, resources, and energy. In the midst of countless articles offering tips and shortcuts, along with various tools and programs that claim to simplify marketing, it's easy to become distracted.

This is the book I wish someone had given me when I began my journey with charities as a volunteer marketing assistant, so I could take the necessary steps to enhance a charity strategy confidently and effectively. From campaign ideas and risk analysis to understanding metrics, building collaboration and support, and turning ideas into actionable steps, this book is intended to be a practical guide. The chapters can stand by themselves, with key information repeated throughout, so you are able to jump in and out of the sections that most resonate with you or where you need the most guidance.

After more than a decade of working with charities, foundations, social enterprises and community groups from diverse sectors, I've come to realise that there is still a lack of easy-to-understand and implement marketing, branding, and communication strategies available to support not-for-profits, especially charities.

People and organisations that genuinely strive to improve individual lives (and society as a whole) continue to be misled by ineffective advice. There is simply no time for that! Witnessing this at close hand, I reached the point where I was compelled to do something. Rather than expanding my consultancy, I decided a better solution was to write a book that would be accessible, manageable and genuinely helpful in guiding efforts of charities - no matter the budget, skill level, or team size.

A bit more about me (and then I promise we'll get to you!).

While studying business at university and not knowing exactly what I wanted to do for a career, I accidentally and absolutely fell in love with the marketing units. 'Sustainability marketing' provided the most enjoyable and satisfying experience of my university years. Although I'd grown up shy of public speaking, I enjoyed giving presentations in this class – marketing for a good purpose – it just made sense to me. If more people knew about the exemplary work being done, more people could get involved and thus increase the impact!

During this time at university, I was also puzzled by this volunteering thing. I couldn't understand why people would pour their heart and soul into a cause that didn't pay them! Until I decided to offer marketing assistance to a community radio station, and then I became instantly hooked.

Despite scarce time and money, the purpose and passion on display from those involved was incredible. Here I must give a shout out to Robyn Tymms, who was really my first mentor in the marketing space. It was conversations with Robyn that would lead me to register a business, become a consultant and mark the start of my marketing career. The team at Iramoo Community Centre in

Melbourne's West trusted me to help them with marketing efforts, as well as joining their Board in a governance perspective. This was my first experience with charity governance, and I was instantly hooked on the ability to make decisions that can affect people's lives and daily experiences for the better.

Over the last fifteen years, there have been a variety of wonderful, challenging, supportive, and purpose-led individuals who have led me to this point, including Glenda Jones who – at my time volunteering for Bacchus Marsh Tourism Association – was a constant reminder of the importance of having a community and audience focus. Glenda was a major inspiration for my continuing efforts in volunteering, community, and marketing for charities.

The work involved to promote a charity's cause is not always easy. However, over the last decade, developing and implementing strategies to assist charities, I've honed my approach to better understand the purpose and community of each organisation I assist, and how to work with them in the most appropriate way.

What has bothered me throughout this time, and still bothers me to this day, is the amount of conflicting information out there, and the number of people in marketing who seem to actively mislead or hinder the progress of charities in achieving meaningful moments for their community.

I'm grateful to have worked across a variety of sectors, including health, education, community and philanthropy; and with and among wonderful people. I've worked with small town charities, start-up social enterprises, industry leaders with a strong charity connection, 'household names', and national campaigns reaching millions of people.

Now I'm sharing with you the framework derived from this experience, in an effort to empower you to unlock your marketing potential, while enabling you to move through the often confusing terrain of advice from 'experts' in the charity arena.

So, why write about marketing?
Funnily enough, marketing appears to have a public relations (PR) problem. There seems to be a barrage of negative sentiment when it comes to marketing, which may not be undeserved, but what about marketing for good? Charities can benefit significantly from a well considered marketing strategy, so let's use this to our advantage and illuminate effective communication opportunities.

This book isn't meant to be a panacea for struggling charities with poor strategic plans, nor is it intended to replace effective fundraising strategies. My goal is that after reading this book, you will have a workable framework and the confidence to both review and optimise an existing marketing strategy, or develop a new one more suitable for your charity.

My mission is to help you showcase your good work, attract more supporters, increase the likelihood of future funding, expand the reach of your campaigns, engage donors and supporters, and cultivate a community that shares your vision.

Designed to be versatile, this book allows you to explore specific sections based on your needs, or follow the framework step by step to develop or audit your marketing strategy. Use it in team meetings, organisation-wide strategy sessions, or one-on-one discussions with key stakeholders, to reflect on your current approach and envision the path forward. Leverage my decade of experience to maximise your impact and outcomes.

Marketing strategy is a broad umbrella term, and as we examine your context and audience, different aspects will come into play, such as branding, communication tactics, and advertising. I'm eager to share the framework I've developed and applied to help charities, foundations, and community groups position themselves to achieve their goals, be it increasing donations, fulfilling partnership agreements or deepening audience connections.

Sadly, I still see many charity leaders and groups continue to make marketing decisions without a tailored strategy, which is understandable given the ever-changing landscape of communication channels and the abundance of self-proclaimed marketing 'gurus'. Further, marketing might not always be the primary focus of an organisation (there I said it) so of course it will never, possibly appropriately receive the same attention as program development, however it at least needs some attention to help your charitable goals.

This 10-part guide offers a straightforward and efficient way to concentrate on marketing without consuming excessive time or resources (you can dive in and out as you need or read the whole thing from start to finish if you're super keen). I'm confident that this framework can be applied to any organisation with the ultimate goal of improving lives. I've seen too many charities and community groups squander time, money, and energy on ineffective strategies. I want to cut through the noise and confusion of the marketing world in a way that resonates clearly and produces a greater impact.

Though I wish I could consult with everyone individually to enhance their organisation's potential, I believe this book is the next best thing. Ultimately, this is my way of giving back to society and creating a better world for future generations.

I'm grateful for the work you do every day, and I hope you find this book useful and enjoyable to read. Together, let's make a difference in the world through strategic marketing and communication. The first step is to get clear on your context.

Why Marketing Matters

1. *Strengthening the Impact of Your Brand*
Branding remains a cornerstone for impact in any business or organisation, with charities being no exception. An effective brand sets your charity apart, forging an emotional connection with your audience, leading to augmented donations, volunteer numbers and engagement. Consistent messaging across all platforms–from your website, social media, and newsletters to brochures and clothing – ensures brand recognition. Your branding should not only be memorable but

also echo the ethos of your charity. Reflect on the message you wish to convey regarding your identity, objectives and reasons for garnering support. Ensuring that your brand aligns with your mission and values is fundamental in order to resonate with your audience, create meaningful moments and establish trust.

2. *Supporting the Lifeblood of Charities*

Fundraising and grants are paramount for most charities. While classic methods like direct mail campaigns retain their value, contemporary marketing techniques can amplify their effect by creating multiple touch points for potential donors or grant makers. Digital marketing stands as a cost-effective conduit to connect with potential donors. Integrating email, content creation, social media, and other online strategies enhances this connection. Social media, with its innate capability to engage, can catalyse donation drives. Delving into data analytics further tailors your efforts, offering insights into donor trends which can shape more targeted campaigns. To sum it up, a holistic marketing approach, merging old and new, magnifies a charity's fundraising outreach.

3. *Confluence of Marketing and Technology*

The digital era has ushered in unparalleled opportunities for charities to amplify their message, expand their supporter base, and hone their campaigns. Data analytics, for instance, provides real-time insights, allowing campaigns to adapt to shifting landscapes. Digital platforms serve as conduits for charities to engage audiences, elevate brand awareness, and foster donor relationships. Automated marketing tools, meanwhile, streamline campaign management, ensuring timely, targeted communication. In essence, marrying marketing and technology equips charities to connect more widely and deeply.

4. Bridging Charities with Audiences

Understanding and connecting with one's audience is vital. Marketing casts a spotlight on a charity's mission, making the unfamiliar familiar to potential supporters, and highlighting why your charity matters to those who already know you and your story. It underscores what differentiates a charity, including why it deserves support. To genuinely resonate, it's crucial to tailor content and marketing approaches to your audience's preferences. Whether it's millennials or another demographic, tapping into current technologies, communication techniques, and trends enhances the efficacy of your message.

In the realm of charity, marketing emerges as a pivotal tool, promising enhanced visibility, deeper donor relationships, and a surge in funds. Navigating the rapidly evolving digital domain is crucial for charities to stay ahead. Beyond mere outreach, marketing often satisfies partnership or funding commitments, marking it as an indispensable element in a charity's success blueprint.

Practical Elements

While navigating through *this book*, you'll stumble upon a few added treasures. I've tucked in 26 marketing ideas, drawn from real-life experiences and tailored for the unique world of charities.

If you've ever wondered about getting your team together to brainstorm and align understandings, there's a guide on setting up your own internal marketing workshop – a little nudge to help everyone get on the same page and share their bright ideas.

And, for those moments when you just want to roll up your sleeves and dive in, there are handy marketing action guides aligned with the framework. They're designed to give you a starting point and a little structure as you weave your charity's unique marketing narrative. Here's hoping these little additions make your journey smoother and a touch more enjoyable.

GETTING CLEAR ON YOUR CONTEXT

Before you focus on developing ideas and strategies relevant to you and your goals, we'll need to pause and take the time to reflect and clarify context. It's tempting to plunge straight into tactics, trends, and tools. But appreciating your current marketing situation is critical for developing an effective and sustainable strategy that will actually help you achieve your goals. As a charity, you will have unique characteristics that can directly affect the effectiveness of your marketing efforts.

One of the first steps in understanding your marketing context is to conduct an audit of your current brand, as well as past communications. While this sounds like a costly and time-draining exercise, the purpose of seeking context isn't to lift every stone and evaluate all previous aspects of your brand. Rather, it's about taking a look at your existing marketing efforts and drawing insight from what is working well, what has worked well in the past, and where you initially think there is room for improvement – thinking about quick wins as well as longer turnaround campaigns or projects that need to happen but are not yet a priority.

In addition to looking at your existing efforts, you'll consider your strengths and weaknesses as a charity. For example, what are your key areas of expertise? What unique value do you bring to the table that sets you apart from other charities? Appreciating your unique strengths will help identify areas where you can focus your marketing efforts.

On the other hand, it's important to identify any challenges that you may face when putting your brand out into the marketplace. In my experience, the most common challenges that appear are limitations to budget, staffing, or volunteer involvement; and/or a lack of experience in certain areas of marketing or communications. By understanding the challenges in moving ideas and action forward, you will be able to develop strategies to overcome these obstacles – ultimately improving your overall marketing effectiveness on broader strategic goals.

Once you have an understanding of your situation and your place in the larger scheme of things, you can develop a strategy that is actually aligned to your vision and mission, moving you towards achieving your goals. This strategy creation stage will include setting specific objectives for your marketing efforts, identifying your key audiences, as well as developing messaging that will resonate with current and potential supporters of your work.

You will need to explore a range of potential channels and tactics, including events, social media, public relations endeavours, email marketing and more. Identify and focus on those that will be most effective in reaching your audience to maximise the impact of your marketing efforts. For the purposes of strategic marketing, the idea is to essentially act as if you are starting from scratch – despite the number of subscribers, database contacts, followers or views you may currently have.

While acknowledging what has and is working from a marketing standpoint, for your strategy to move on a growth trajectory, we'll need to try to be open to change. There is no need to delete your current profiles, stop writing your newsletter or throw away all your marketing material – just keep your mind open as you plan what to do moving forward. Out of this process you will be able to incorporate what is working successfully into your strategic marketing approach.

As you approach a strategic marketing position, be prepared to bring measurement and evaluation into play early. This can include tracking metrics such as website traffic, donation numbers, content shareability, positive social media engagement, email open rates, and using the most relevant data to adjust your strategy as needed. It's important to continuously evaluate and adjust the strategy based on the results seen (or any unintended consequences that arise).

So, let's get started.

Strategic Objective Alignment

As a charity, having a strong marketing strategy is essential for achieving your goals. However, before you can develop an effective strategy, you need to first link your marketing goals to your strategic objectives. By doing so, you create a tool for context focus to ensure that your marketing efforts and outcomes are aligned with the overall vision and mission of your work.

Let's look at some examples to illustrate this. One fairly well known international organisation that's doing an exceptional job at linking marketing goals to strategic objectives is Water.org. The organisation's mission is to provide access to safe water and sanitation to people in need all around the world.

To achieve this goal, *Water.org* has created a comprehensive strategy that focuses on raising awareness of the brand, engaging supporters in the work that is being done (and the work that still needs doing) and driving donations.

One of Water.org's key marketing goals is to increase the number of people who are aware of the global water crisis and the impact the lack of safe water access and sanitation can have on individuals and communities. By increasing awareness of this key message, *Water.org* can attract new supporters, partners and donors who are passionate about their cause and driven to support it.

To this end, *Water.org* has implemented a range of tactics that are aligned to their strategic goal. For example, through their selected social media channels, email newsletters and website as the core content hub, they regularly share stories and photos of the people they have assisted.

Another great example of a charity linking marketing goals to strategic objectives is *Save the Children*. Its mission to improve the lives of children around the world is supported by an effective strategy to help achieve this goal.

One of Save the Children's key marketing goals is to raise funds (yes, actual money – not likes or followers) to support their programs and services. By raising funds, the organisation can expand their reach of operations and help more children in need.

To develop this marketing strategy, Save the Children has clearly identified the tactics most relevant to their message and their audience or community. For example, they regularly send out fundraising appeals through direct email, email newsletters and social media campaigns. To tie it all together, they also host fundraising events and partner with corporate sponsors to generate donations.

These examples highlight the importance of linking marketing goals to key objectives in order to ensure context clarity and strategic alignment. By doing so, you can develop a marketing strategy that is tailored to your unique mission and goals.

Four initial thinking points for linking your marketing goals to strategic objectives include:

- *Does your strategic plan have clear and measurable goals? Let's transfer these to marketing!*

  Defining clear and measurable goals that align with your existing strategic plan, vision and mission is a crucial step towards a successful marketing strategy that makes a positive impact for your work. These goals should be specific, measurable, attainable, relevant, and time-bound (*SMART*). By setting SMART goals, you can monitor your progress and adjust your strategy accordingly. For example, if your charity's strategic goal is to increase fundraising by 20% in the next year, your marketing goal might be to create a targeted email campaign that will generate a 5% increase in donations within the next three months.

- *Who would you consider to be your primary audience and what do they want to hear from you?*

  Identifying your audiences or community and developing meaningful messages that will resonate with them is another important component of a successful marketing strategy. Understanding your audience's needs, interests, and preferences will help you tailor your messaging and make a deeper connection with them. Once you have a better understanding of your current audience, you can develop key messages that will resonate with them.

- *Looking at your primary audience (yes, again) – where do they receive other marketing messages?*

  Identifying the channels and approaches that will be most effective in reaching your audience is another critical step. There are many different options available, including social media, email marketing, website content, events and public relations. It's important to identify those methods that will be most effective in reaching your audience, based on their preferences, behaviour and what their 'day to day' life looks like.

- *How do you measure the degree to which a message resonates with our audience?*

  Evaluating and adjusting your marketing based on results and feedback is crucial to ensure that your strategy remains effective and relevant over time. Regularly tracking and analysing your metrics, such as engagement rates, click-through rates, and donations generated, can help you identify what's working and what's not – it helps you identify if your message is reaching your intended audience and if they are motivated to take action. Additionally, asking for feedback from your audience and team members can provide valuable insights and help you make informed decisions about your communication strategy. Based on these insights, you can adjust your strategy as needed to ensure that it remains effective and well targeted in achieving your objectives.

Audience and Message

The first step in this framework is mapping your specific context, conscious of your intended audience and message. This will allow us to build a strategy specific to you and what makes your charity unique. No, I am not suggesting a SWOT analysis! Although this is certainly useful, it can tend to feel like a mandatory chore.

Essentially, you want to create a guiding light for your marketing work, whether it be small communication tactical decisions, significant presentation pitches to potential funders, or casual conversation at an industry or community event.

Understanding your context means thinking about your primary audience of today, looking at your vision, and mapping how this will change over the next ten years. Beginning with a very practical element, let's survey real people – including people who don't know about you, people who know you by name, people who have already engaged with you and people who are connected to the organisation. Of course there are already numerous survey companies doing solid work and providing extensive analysis, but the approach here is different.

Let's think about exactly what to include in a survey (or poll) for each of these groups. Ideally there should be no more than 3 questions in each as a starting point for context mapping. The vehicle of your survey (how people will complete it) will ideally match how you're currently speaking with them. Is it a phone, email newsletter, in person when they visit? I'm not going to pretend I know the answer to that question... It's about trusting your initial judgement about how you talk with your charity's audience currently.

Okay, so understanding your actual context relies on other people's points of view, not on what is written in your organisation's strategic plan. This will give us a glimpse into the lives of the real humans we want to care about our mission, as opposed to fictional personas. Once these polls have been conducted, opportunities and challenges will be revealed. Set a 20-minute meeting to look at how the results marry up with your public facing purpose and action. This process will allow gaps to become apparent – findings can be noted down in a useful one pager.

You will build one smart poll for use with everyone. However each person's first answer will determine which particular group they are segmented into. This means there is one survey to promote, one deadline and one set of dates.

First, list your top five promotional methods. Then, conduct a websearch on the organisation that you consider to be your biggest competitor in the space. Notice what they seem to have to promote their messaging. Consider anything they are using that is not on your list, and add it to your 'worth a look at' pile for now.

Select which promotional methods are relevant to each type of audience – below is a list of suggestions as a starting point for you to adapt.

People who don't know about you

- If budget permits, some paid advertising.
- If not, include a section at the end of the survey giving people the opportunity to share to their network.

- Attend a local community event.
- Spend 20 minutes vox-popping people down the street.

People who know you by name

- Friends.
- Family.
- Your LinkedIn network.
- Your Facebook page.
- Include a section at the end of the survey giving people the opportunity to share to their network.

People who have previously engaged with you

- Website notice.
- Email newsletter.
- Include a section at the end of the survey giving people the opportunity to share their network. People close to the organisation are likely to share it to their network and this will put the poll in front of people who have never heard of you and your goals.

People who are connected to your charity (stakeholders).

- Internal email.
- Staff meetings.
- Intranet.
- Competition.
- Strategy day.

- Stakeholder invoices.
- Annual General Meeting.

Use your existing channels to promote your survey for at least one week. Then check for results and adjust as necessary.

Meanwhile, spend time in your team (or in self reflection) thinking about the following:

- List three things you consider are unique to your charity, and three pain points you have (that are most likely common in the charity sector). This will help with idea generation, but also contribute to context mapping (context-ception anyone)?
- What have you found to be successful in marketing to date?
- What things didn't work?
- What's an idea you've had (maybe from left field) that never came up at a meeting as an option?

After the poll has been out for a week, check the feedback to gather data points. If you're not getting responses, is there anything you can do to incentivise people, such as a competition or random giveaway (any merch laying around)?

While week two of the poll gets underway, a critical element of context mapping is actually messaging. Make sure this is clear. If asked what you are trying to achieve, would you simply regurgitate your mission statement? If you think about the last person you spoke to about your charity, did you do this? Or maybe you focused on a specific story of impact or part of your vision for the future, or some upcoming projects?

Broadcast Exercise

If you had the chance to broadcast 30 seconds to every single person in the population, what would you say? How would you act? Let's forget about segmentation for now and keep it general – this message goes to everyone.

Everyone hears the message at the same time? Let's do that right now! Turn on your phone's camera or voice recorder, write the first three dot points you would like to communicate, and without notice take the opportunity to tell the world about your purpose as a charity.
Record, and listen back to what you've said.

Did you include a call to action? Did you incorporate a story from your work? Did you leave out any buzzwords that might confuse someone who doesn't know about you? Did you thank key partners? Reflect for five minutes on what you could have included to make the most of that broadcast.

Then, do that exercise again, but this time placing in front of mind that when this broadcast goes out, it's a major intrusion into everyone's lives and they are patiently waiting for your broadcast to be over so they can get back to their own personal goals. Let's turn on that phone recording and go again. What did you say?

Write these two scripts – cool messaging and hot messaging – in your context map (computer document or notepad, whatever you're used to at the moment), and pick out only the elements which appeared in both. Then you can draft a one sentence message that is your core purpose. This is the impact we want to boost with an improved marketing strategy and tactics.

Now let's examine the survey results. If you're using a free tool like *Survey Monkey* or *Google forms,* you'll get some clear reports that you can reflect on to fine tune your context map. By now, you should have the following: your cool messaging, your hot messaging and the output statement.

The Brand Conversation

Branding is an essential part of any successful marketing strategy, and this holds true for charities as well. Creating a strong and consistent brand identity can help your charity stand out in a crowded marketplace and make a lasting impression on your audience. Here's a quick checklist to work your way through branding 101 to build a solid foundation for our marketing.

Define Your Brand Values:
Your brand values should be at the core of your communication and marketing strategy. They define who you are, what you stand for, and how you approach your mission. Take the time to articulate your brand values and ensure that they are reflected in all aspects of your communication approach.

Develop a Visual Identity:
A strong visual identity can help your charity create a recognisable and consistent brand image. This includes things like your logo, colour palette, typography and imagery. Develop a set of visual guidelines that can be used by your team and any external partners to ensure consistency across all communication channels.

Craft Your Messaging:
Your messaging should be clear, concise and consistent across all communication channels. Develop key messages that resonate with your target audience and reinforce your brand values. These messages should be used consistently across all communication channels, from social media to email marketing to events.

Create a Content Strategy:
A content strategy can help you build a consistent brand identity across all your communication channels. Develop a plan for the type of content you will create and the channels you will use for distribution. This should include a mix of original content and curated content that is relevant to your audience.

Leverage Social Media:
Social media is an important tool for building your brand and engaging with your audience. Develop a social media strategy that aligns with your brand values and messaging, and be sure to use visuals and storytelling to make your posts more engaging.

Build Relationships with Stakeholders and Influencers:
Influential stakeholders and industry-relevant influencers can help you reach new audiences

and build your brand. Identify influencers in your space who align with your brand values and mission, and build relationships with them. Collaborate on content or events to build a mutually beneficial relationship.

Measure Your Brand Impact:
To understand the impact of your brand, you need to measure it. Develop metrics that track the success of your branding efforts, such as brand awareness, engagement and sentiment. Use these metrics to evaluate the success of your branding efforts and make adjustments as needed.

Summary
Before you focus on developing ideas and strategies relevant to you and your goals, take the time to reflect and clarify your context. It will be worth it in the long run! Appreciating your current marketing situation is critical for developing an effective and sustainable strategy that will actually help you achieve your goals.

Conducting an audit will allow you to look at your existing marketing efforts and gain insights about what is working well and where you initially think there is room for improvement. Identifying your unique strengths will help point you towards the best focus for your marketing efforts.

Ensure you link your marketing goals to your strategic objectives. By doing so, you ensure that your marketing efforts and outcomes are aligned with the overall vision and mission of your work. To understand your context properly you need to connect with real people, not just refer to your organisation's strategic plan or historical documents. Think about your primary audience and look at your vision to help map the way forward.

Workshopping with hot messaging and cold messaging will help you create a one sentence output statement summarising your core purpose. Creating a strong and consistent brand identity will also help your charity stand out in a crowded marketplace and make a lasting impression on your audience.

Action Guide:
Brand and Marketing Audit

Overview

This worksheet is designed to help charities evaluate their current branding and communication strategies, identifying key aspects to consider. Use this document to pinpoint focus areas and create a plan for strengthening your brand and communication efforts.

What is working?

a. List the top 3-5 aspects of your brand/marketing/communication that have been successful.

b. Explain why these aspects have been successful (eg. clear messaging, strong visuals, effective targeting).

What is not working?

a. List the 3-5 aspects of your brand/communication that have yet to be successful.

b. Explain why you think these aspects have yet to be successful (eg. lack of consistency, unclear messaging, poor targeting).

What do we need to eliminate?

a. Identify any aspects of your brand/marketing/communication that are no longer relevant or effective.

b. Explain why these aspects should be eliminated (eg. outdated design, negative associations, lack of impact).

What do we need to reduce?

a. Identify any aspects of your brand/communication that may be over-emphasised or need to be clarified.

b. Explain why these aspects should be reduced (eg. diluting core messaging, causing brand clutter, diminishing returns).

What ideas do we need to refine?

a. List any concepts or strategies that have potential but require further development.
b. Describe how these ideas can be improved (e.g., clarifying messaging, strengthening visuals, better targeting).

Other prompts

a. *Competitor analysis:* Identify your top 2 competitors and analyse their branding/communication strategies, as well as their channels used and content developed. What can you learn from their successes and failures?
b. *Target audience:* Re-evaluate your target audience to ensure your messaging reaches the right people. Are there any segments you may be overlooking or under-emphasising?
c. *Content audit:* Review your existing content (website, social media, marketing materials) for consistency, relevance, and effectiveness. Make a plan to update or remove outdated or ineffective content.
d. *Metrics and measurement:* Identify the key performance indicators (KPIs) for your brand/

communication efforts. Establish a system for tracking and analysing these metrics to inform future decisions.

After completing this worksheet, use the insights gathered to create a plan of action for improving your brand and communication efforts. Regularly review and update your strategies to ensure continued success and growth.

SYSTEM TO GENERATE (GOOD) MARKETING IDEAS

Inspiration

While it's important to have a clear picture of what you do and how you'd like to move forward, be careful not to get stuck at the planning stage. On the other hand, plunging straight into ideas to improve your marketing efforts will increase the risk of spending time, energy and money on something not leading to a purpose-led outcome. This can be a tricky balancing act.

If you spend little or no time on context mapping, or alternately, too much time focusing on planning details, you are likely to generate unproductive ideas. What do I mean by ideas? I'm talking about any concept, innovation, campaign, or thought that you and your team can employ to move your marketing forward and achieve your goals.

I would like to share two personal examples with you, which while embarrassing, illustrate how

I came to understand this balance of ideas. At the time I worked with a purpose-led health organisation, surrounded by really great people who were trusting me to come up with solutions to grow their brand recognition in their community. As a marketer with some wins on the board, I thought I could apply ideas that had worked elsewhere. I drew up a strategy which sounded good and looked at everything I thought could be created or improved, based on my previous ideas and experience.

A month later my strategy was ready to be presented to the executive team. However I started to have second thoughts after speaking directly with the organisation's key audience (their community) in literally the hallways while they waited for an appointment. I realised this plan would not work and decided to scrap the whole thing. It was simply 'too corporate', missing the human element and local understanding.

To create context properly, I then surveyed those impacted by marketing decisions and the direction of the organisation to obtain their points of view. This direct feedback resulted in a completely new, effective strategy that was more about health education and the service's historical significance. The process of speaking directly to these people also gave me a deeper insight into the local terminology, concerns and understanding of the brand – all of which affect messaging moving forward. Having a one pager context explainer for your charity and cause also provides an easy-to-view document for stakeholders to obtain quick feedback if desired.

Let's now look at how you can generate ideas that match your context and how to quickly test these ideas to ensure goal alignment.

Inspiration is not something that you can allocate specific time for – inspiration cannot be forced, but it is beneficial to have some avenue, or focus of sorts, each day to help new ideas flow. Different things work for different people, however I have found it helpful to 'prime my brain' in the morning to inspire new marketing ideas and identify communication solutions. You might already be doing this, possibly even subconsciously. And the fact that you're seeking information from this book, will hopefully be a source of inspiration for you as well as providing guidance.

Here is one idea to see if it resonates with you (you be the judge if it is a good or bad idea): at the start of the day think about what you hope to achieve, for example 'I will think of a unique idea to match my marketing goals'. Once you have this thought primed, let it go, so there is no feeling of pressure. It's okay if the desired inspiration does not arrive today or tomorrow, but it might work in the back of your mind while you are doing other things.

Funnily enough, I have found it much more productive to not always have a marketing lens switched on. When I'm going for a walk or commuting, rather than listening to a marketing podcast, I will listen to a history or education podcast. Then I often find that I am able to come back to a 'marketing problem' with ideas or concepts. Part of this is also having a set way to quickly capture the ideas that pop into your head, so you don't lose them. This really depends on what works with you. I've tried note taking apps but they don't seem to work so well with me, so I like making an audio recording of the idea or even sending an email to myself (using a quick compose email shortcut on my phone).

While there are many great hosts out there, if you are leaning heavily on marketing podcasts, I suggest putting in time on other interest areas, or areas you have not explored before - things that could work for you just by being included in your day, without adding any extra burden.

Instead of *Twitter/X or Facebook*, engage with sites like *Trust Cafe* (the social network created by Wikipedia Founder Jimmy Wales or *Reddit* (where you can quickly get across innovation happening from around the world) to break your normal social media routine.

For inspiration, in this book I've included a Marketing Toolbox of 26 marketing and communication ideas that I have found to be useful for charities and causes. Now, that's of course way too many to implement at once. Some might resonate and some might not, but an interesting exercise is to select five you think you might like to try over the next 12 months, just based on your intuition.

These toolbox ideas are not hard and fast instructions or rules about what can work. There will be elements of these ideas that will be transferable to your current context, or perhaps you can use them as a launching pad.

One thing that really annoys me is when someone comes into an organisation and immediately suggests an idea that will definitely work. How could they possibly know that without understanding the organisation's context?

But why 26 ideas in the toolbox?

The structure of 26 ideas provides one idea a fortnight (for the super eager) to focus on. Think about whether an idea makes sense for you in your context and based on the suggested criteria. But don't become overwhelmed by trying to take on board too much too quickly.

Sitting with an idea, testing it, talking about it and having it as part of conversations – this will prime your brain to keep an eye out for things that are happening externally, signalling whether this is a good fit for your mission or not.

Even if your initial reaction to an idea is 'Oh, that's not for us', don't necessarily dismiss it out of hand. It may be a cue to think about what elements could work for you, and it may be worthwhile including it in your five ideas to explore.

The toolbox breaks each idea down into short sections - the first step towards incorporating the idea into your marketing strategy, a traditional approach to how you could action the idea, a 'push the limits' version for those with a greater risk tolerance, and of course an example of a success indicator.

Fast, Focussed Idea Testing

Idea sessions and idea focus time can of course take many forms. In my experience the most effective is to select a group of 2-7 people who you trust and who have the values of the charity at heart. Ask if they would like to be involved in an ideas session to improve the success of your marketing and communication ventures. This doesn't need to be the whole executive team or the communications and fundraising team; or volunteers. We are looking for a mix of people here, ideally something like this:

- Has known the mission for less than a year.
- Has known the mission for more than a year.
- Has detailed experience within the sector.
- Has detailed experience outside the current sector.
- An artist/musician/creative.
- Is someone active on social media and across latest trends.

The exercise consists of generating ideas fairly quickly, the purpose being to make the organisation's marketing strategy more effective.

Before setting up the session, ask each participant to respond to these four simple prompts:

- What unexpected trend will we see in 3 years?
- What's the most ridiculous thing our charity could do next month?
- If we won an innovation award next year, what could it be for?
- How could we improve with a $500,000 grant delivered tomorrow?

While you may not have such large sums at your disposal, expensive marketing ideas often have less expensive variations, which could be implemented on a smaller scale and still be effective.

Give this group a week to respond – this can be done by pen/paper, google forms, survey monkey, email, whatever you think is the most likely way someone will get back to you. You might even gather responses by having an informal conversation with someone over a coffee. If so, ask permission to record the questions and answers so you don't disrupt the flow of conversation by frantically writing notes down.

Once you have feedback (and if someone is delaying or unlikely to provide feedback at all, please find someone else to fill their spot), set up a face-to-face meeting. It works best if it's around 30 minutes with a tight agenda – example below

– and works even better if it's off site, somewhere new to everyone. Of course this will be dependent on what works for you; it's not always possible to take everyone off site.

Example agenda

- Introduction – thank you and purpose (4 minutes).
- Reflection by each person on the prompt questions and their answers (8 minutes).
- Shared responses – for each prompt question, ask for a volunteer to share their response (8 minutes).
- Discussion specifically around marketing or campaign ideas they'd like to see implemented (10 minutes).

The discussion time will help hone people's thoughts and provide a pool of ideas. From these, select three ideas to test, based on your context.

Quick testing can be done many ways – pick out a few that resonate with you and your available time, and are likely to have the greatest reach across the range of charity stakeholders. Of course, buy-in from the broader audience is important as well.

- All staff email (usually has to be from the CEO to have affect).
- Live poll at the staff meeting.

- Live poll at the Annual General Meeting.
- Survey for email newsletter subscribers (please avoid doing this on social media).
- Marker sheet at your front desk if you have one.
- Direct email to some of your suppliers, stakeholders or long term donors.

In order to test these ideas quickly, only ask one question at this stage: If we (insert idea here) would it help us achieve our goals? Yes or No.

Selecting a Marketing Idea

This is a discovery stage. Once you've generated at least three ideas, just sit with those ideas. You don't need to rush into implementing them. That would risk breaking things, failing forward and all that – in many cases in this sector, there isn't the luxury to 'break things' and take learnings... we need some marketing wins! Give yourselves some time with these ideas, some space. Settle for a couple of days, and then start looking around to see what is being talked about relevant to the ideas that resonate the most with you here. What else is being talked about in relation to these topics on your favourite social networking or news source site?

Once you begin evaluating each idea broadly – with no focus in particular – you are going to narrow down the ideas to the one you want to try first, placing the other two in the 'to be assessed again later' pile.

Once you have your primary idea that you think, on your best judgement, could work in your context and based on the inspiration and discovery you've done up until now, look at how you can 'score' each idea. Give each idea one tick based on the following 8 prompts. The idea with the most ticks is the one you will take to the next step.

- Will this idea, if successful, have a positive flow on affect to your overall objectives?
- Can this idea be done with $0 and in less than one hour?
- Can this idea be done with $500 and in less than one day?
- Can we do this idea internally without hiring someone?
- Can you explain the idea in one sentence?
- Can you summarise the idea in three words?
- Is this the first time we are trying something like this?
- Are you confident the idea could be implemented in one month?

The idea with the most ticks will allow you to progress to the phases of justification and testing. The justification step will vary widely in the way it looks, depending on who you are – whether you're a founder, board member or part of a fundraising team. For example, as a board member you may wish to cross-check your idea with the company director guidelines. From my experience, justification is really nailing down how the idea links to your overall purpose and context, and providing internal (and sometimes external) stakeholder confidence. To do this, you need to bring evaluation into the conversation early. The *Australian Institute of Company Directors* has great resources on the role of governance and marketing, and the *Institute of Community Directors Australia* for charity directors.

I love audience surveys. Whether it's pen/paper surveys, a staff lunch, online surveys or events to get to know the people you're trying to market to. At the core of audience connection is bringing together the people who are closest to any impact of this idea (positive, neutral or negative), including looking at potential unintended consequences. The unintended consequences of your actions can outweigh any or all of the positive impacts from your marketing strategy.

What do you want to see as a result of this idea and when? Clarify your specific goals and evaluation criteria. Importantly, what could offset your gains? If you set a goal to increase reach so more potential donors know about the cause, you want to make sure they're actually paying attention to the content. Therefore you measure by engagement. However, if your content gets negative reviews, the hoped-for impact will be offset and the strategy may have a shorter life than you anticipated. Another example is 'web traffic' – what if people are going to the wrong page, or leaving the page as soon as they get there?

Once again, focus on exactly what you want to achieve from this idea that will turn into marketing and communication action? What is the main thing? Organisations that rely heavily on 'brand awareness' or 'reach' as the main evaluation technique of marketing ideas may be measuring the wrong things. Even 'engagement' is questionable without context. One million negative comments demonstrates high engagement, but not great results for your brand and your ability to reach the goals outlined in your strategic plan.

What are the mechanisms involved when we look at how we will evaluate this idea and after what specified period of time?

10 Minute Activity
What are three sentences you would love to include in your next Annual Report or Impact Statement about this idea?

Imagine the idea was a complete success with no unintended consequences and there has been plenty of positive audience feedback about the approach.

Then, imagine that the idea didn't work. Even though your idea didn't reach your original evaluation goals and it wasn't the success you hoped it would be, what was the worst outcome that resulted? What improvements regarding your marketing and communications could you take away from that? Write three sentences based on this alternate scenario.

These deliberations will point your marketing decisions towards achieving your broader goals and purpose.

Summary

It is important to have a clear picture of what you do and how you'd like to move forward, before plunging straight into trying new ideas. But be careful also, not to get stuck in the planning stage. This can be a tricky balancing act.

While inspiration cannot be forced, it is beneficial to have some avenue, or focus of sorts, each day to help new ideas flow. The list of toolbox strategies provided in this book is not a set of hard and fast instructions or rules about what can work. There will be elements of these ideas that will be transferable to your current context, or perhaps you can use them as a launching pad.

You need to determine whether an idea makes sense for you in your context. Sitting with an idea, testing it, talking about it and having it as part of conversations will help you notice things that are happening externally, signalling whether this is a good fit for your mission or not. Selecting one idea to focus on involves a discovery process.

Clarify your specific goals and evaluation criteria. In addition, think about what could offset your gains. These deliberations will inform your marketing decisions towards achieving your broader goals and purpose.

Action Guide:
Prompts for Marketing Ideas

Overview

This worksheet is designed to guide charities in conducting meetings or workshops aimed at generating marketing ideas that are genuinely relevant to their goals, audience, and context. By following these prompts, you can foster an environment that encourages creativity and collaboration while maintaining focus on strategic needs.

Meeting/Workshop Preparation

a. Define the purpose and objectives of the meeting/workshop (e.g., brainstorming new marketing campaign ideas, refining communication strategies).

b. Identify the key stakeholders and participants (eg. marketing team, leadership, external consultants).

c. Prepare relevant background materials, data, and insights (eg. target audience profiles, competitor analysis, industry trends).

Icebreaker Activity

Choose a brief, engaging activity to warm up participants and encourage open communication.

Consider activities that promote collaboration, creativity and a relaxed atmosphere.

Context Setting

Highlight any specific challenges, opportunities, or constraints that should be considered during the idea generation process.

Prompts for Generating Relevant Ideas

a. What are our target audience's key needs, wants, and interest areas or cause areas that have a personal impact'? How can our marketing address these?

b. How can our communication directly impact our charity goals? What actions do we need to take to address this?

c. How can we measure the success of our marketing efforts about our goals?

d. What current industry trends or market conditions should we consider when developing our communication?

e. How can we differentiate our marketing efforts from those of our competitors?

f. Are there any barriers that may affect our communication efforts, and how can we address them?

Encourage participants to brainstorm marketing ideas. Capture all ideas, regardless of initial feasibility or perceived value. After the brainstorming session, work together to evaluate and prioritise ideas based on their relevance to the objectives, target audience, and context. Identify any areas where further research, refinement, or development is needed.

Action Guide: Decision Making Framework

Overview

This worksheet is designed to help charities create a decision-making framework for evaluating and ranking communication ideas. By completing this worksheet, you can establish criteria for determining the quality of comms ideas and prioritise them based *on their potential impact and alignment with your strategic goals.*

Define Evaluation Criteria

a. List the key factors that contribute to the success of a marketing idea (eg, audience relevance, message clarity, creativity, cost-effectiveness, scalability).

b. For each factor, briefly describe what it entails and why it is important for your charity.

Create a Rating Scale

Write a rating scale, ranging from 1 (poor) to 5 (excellent). Provide guidelines for the rankings.

Communications Ideas Inventory

List all the communication ideas you would like to evaluate. Describe each idea - objectives, target audience, content, etc.

Rate Marketing Ideas

Using the rating scale from 3, rate each communication idea in 4.

Rank Marketing Ideas

Sort the communication ideas based on their total scores, highest to lowest.

Idea Prioritisation and Selection

a. Based on the rankings from 6, select the top communication ideas to implement.

b. Identify why the lowest ranking ideas require further research, refinement, or development.

Implementation Plan

For each prioritised communication idea, outline the steps needed for successful implementation. Assign responsibilities, deadlines, and resources for each step.

Monitoring and Evaluation

a. Identify key performance indicators (KPIs) for each communication idea to measure its effectiveness in achieving your goals.

b. Establish a system for tracking and analysing the outcomes to inform future decisions and adjustments.

FINDING THE TIME (OR NOT)

While there is guidance throughout the rest of this book on how to achieve effective marketing no matter how much time you have available, there are three things to keep in mind to help streamline your activities if you're strapped for time - focusing on time critical events that your charity is focused on anyway, engage in broader national conversations, and remember any marketing contractual obligations to funders or partners.

Time Critical Events

Effective marketing and communication is critical to the success of any charity, but it can be challenging to manage in the midst of busy schedules and competing priorities.

One key strategy to ensure that your efforts are effective is to map out time-critical communication events in advance. Mapping out these events helps you prioritise and plan your communication efforts so that you can maximise their impact. By identifying the events that are most important to your organisation and allocating resources accordingly, you can ensure that your message is well-planned and prepared for greatest effectiveness.

For example, let's say your charity is hosting a fundraising event in a few months. This event will be critical to your organisation's financial success for the year, so you need to ensure that your communication efforts leading up to the event are strategic and effective.

To begin mapping out your communication strategy, start by identifying the key milestones leading up to the event. These might include things like the announcement of the event, the opening of ticket sales, and reminders leading up to the event. Next, consider the target audience for each milestone. Who do you want to reach with each message, and what do you want them to do as a result?

Once you've identified your milestones and target audience, it's time to plan your communication tactics. What channels will you use to reach your audience? Will you use social media, email, direct mail, or a combination of these? How frequently will you communicate with your audience, and what messages will you send?

As you plan your time critical strategy, be sure to set measurable goals for each milestone. How many tickets do you want to sell, and by what date? How many social media followers do you want to gain, and how quickly? By setting clear goals and tracking your progress, you can ensure that your communication efforts are effective and that you're making the most of your resources.

Of course, it's not just fundraising events that require careful planning. Other time-critical communication events might include the launch of a new program, the release of a report or a response to a crisis. For each event, it's essential to identify the key milestones, target audience, and communication tactics to ensure that your message is received and acted upon.

Consider how your communication efforts align with your overall strategic goals. If your charity's goal is to increase awareness of a particular issue, your communication efforts should be focused on reaching a broad audience and educating them about the issue. On the other hand, if your goal is to recruit volunteers for a specific program, your communication efforts should be targeted to a more specific audience.

The most important thing to note is always make charity events that are time critical part of any planning documents or content schedule, to ensure it's front of mind and you can begin to not only work backwards to identify relevant marketing activities, but you can also piece together any collaboration or content options that tie into a broader conversation.

The Broader Conversation

Charities often have important messages to share with their audience, but sometimes those messages can get lost in the noise of everyday life. One way to amplify your message is to connect it to significant national and international events. These events provide a platform for your organisation to engage meaningfully with your audience on a larger scale.

In Australia, there are a number of significant national events that charities can link their communications with. ANZAC Day is a day of remembrance for Australians and New Zealanders who have served and died in wars, conflicts and peacekeeping operations. For charities focused on veterans' issues or mental health, ANZAC

Day provides an opportunity to springboard communications that connect with the sentiments of the day, such as through sharing stories of veterans and raising awareness about mental health support services.

Cancer Research UK has connected its marketing to various global events, such as Breast Cancer Awareness Month in October and World Cancer Day in February. These events provide an opportunity for the charity to leverage off broader publicity in order to raise awareness about the importance of cancer research and encourage people to support their work.

Amnesty International has connected its marketing to International Women's Day, a global event that takes place every year on March 8th. Amnesty International uses this event to highlight the struggles faced by women around the world and to promote its work in defending human rights.

WaterAid has connected its marketing to World Water Day, a global event that takes place every year on March 22nd. World Water Day focuses on the importance of fresh water and sustainable water management. WaterAid uses this event as an opportunity to publicise the global water crisis and promote their work in providing clean water and sanitation to communities in need.

Connecting communication content to significant national events is a powerful way to engage with your audience and tailor your message. By choosing events that align with your organisation's values and mission, you can create a powerful connection with your audience and build a stronger sense of community around your cause.

When connecting your communication content to national events in this way, it's important to consider the tone and messaging of your content. Avoid appropriating or co-opting the event for your own purposes, and instead focus on how your organisation can contribute to the cause in a meaningful way. You can also consider partnering with other organisations to amplify your message and reach a larger audience.

Ideally, you're not just posting to social media on the day, but work the date significantly broader into your strategy, ongoing communications, and activities. These dates also offer an opportunity to connect with like-minded charities and causes to share the same message and cross pollinate each other's audiences.

Meeting Obligations

It's no surprise to you that charities often rely on funding from partners or funders to support their programs and initiatives. In return, these partners or funders may require certain contractual obligations to be met by the charity. Meeting these obligations is not only important for maintaining a positive relationship with the funder, but also for the continued success of the charity's programs.

One way to ensure that contractual obligations are met is by scheduling time in your charity's marketing and communications calendar to deliver on these obligations. This ensures that these obligations are not forgotten or neglected amidst other priorities and allows the charity to plan ahead and allocate resources appropriately.

Establish clear communication channels with your partners or funders to promote positive collaborative relationships. For instance, a common contractual obligation that a charity has is to provide regular progress reports to their funders. By scheduling regular check-ins and reports, the charity can ensure that they are meeting their obligation while also providing valuable updates to the funder on the progress of their programs, and allowing for open and honest communication about any challenges or delays that may arise.

Remember to acknowledge the contribution of a partner or funder in your charity's marketing materials, whether on your website or in promotional materials. By scheduling time to create and publish these acknowledgements, the charity can demonstrate their appreciation for the support they have received while also fulfilling their contractual obligation.

It is worthwhile designating a person or team to be responsible for managing and delivering on contractual obligations. This ensures that there is a clear point of contact for the partner or funder and demonstrates that the obligation is being prioritised within the charity.

Finally, charities can use project management tools or software to track progress on their contractual obligations and ensure that they are being delivered on time. This allows for easy monitoring of deadlines and progress, as well as the ability to quickly identify and address any delays or issues that arise.

Summary

Effective communication is crucial to the success of any charity's marketing efforts.

However, with limited resources and competing priorities, finding the time for communications can be a challenge. Mapping out time-critical communication events for your charity in advance – fundraising events, program launches or other important dates that require communication to stakeholders – allows you to plan your communications and ensure that you have the time and resources needed to execute them effectively.

You can also connect your content to significant national or international events. For example, if your charity works on environmental issues, you could plan a communication campaign around Earth Day or World Environment Day. By linking your communication to national events, you can capitalise on existing momentum and increase the visibility of your message.

It's also important to schedule time to deliver any contractual obligations to partners or funders, such as delivering necessary updates and reports. This will ensure that you maintain positive relationships with your partners and funders.

Action Guide: Sell your Marketing Strategy

Overview

This worksheet is designed to help you brainstorm and plan an effective pitch for presenting marketing ideas and strategies to stakeholders or team members, in person or by email. By completing this worksheet, you can create a compelling and persuasive presentation that increases the likelihood of approval and internal buy-in.

Define the Objective

a. Clearly define the purpose of the pitch/email (eg. to gain approval for a communication strategy, to secure resources for a new campaign).

b. Identify the key stakeholders or recipients of the pitch/email (eg. management, team members, other departments).

Clarify the Idea or Strategy

a. Provide a brief overview of the marketing idea or strategy, including its objectives, target audience, and proposed messaging or content.

b. Explain how this idea or strategy aligns with the charity's overall goals and priorities.

Establish Credibility

a. Highlight any relevant research, data, or insights that support the effectiveness of the proposed idea or strategy (eg. audience insights, industry trends, case studies).

b. Showcase any past successes or experiences that demonstrate your ability to execute the proposed idea or strategy effectively.

Address Concerns and Objections

a. Anticipate any potential concerns or objections that stakeholders might have (eg. cost, feasibility, risks).

b. Develop clear and concise responses to address these concerns, emphasising the value and benefits of the proposed idea or strategy.

Demonstrate Impact and ROI

a. Clearly outline the expected outcomes and benefits of the proposed idea or strategy (eg. increased brand awareness, improved customer engagement, higher sales).

b. Provide estimates of the return on investment (ROI) or other key performance indicators (KPIs) to help quantify the potential impact and value of the idea or strategy.

Outline the Implementation Plan

Break down the proposed idea or strategy into actionable steps, including any necessary tasks, resources, and deadlines. Make a clear plan of execution.

Call to Action

Clearly state the specific actions or decisions you are requesting from stakeholders (eg. approval, resource allocation, input, collaboration, and deadlines).

After completing this worksheet, you should have a well-planned and compelling pitch for presenting your communication ideas to stakeholders. Use this plan to secure approval and internal buy-in, enabling your charity to move forward with effective and impactful communication initiatives.

Remember to keep your completed worksheet for future reference, and revisit the steps as needed to refine and adapt your pitch or email for different ideas, strategies, or audiences.

PREPARING EARLY FOR EVALUATION

Early Evaluation

Effective communication and marketing strategies are crucial for charities to reach their goals and achieve their missions. However, it's not enough to create and implement a plan; it's equally important to evaluate its effectiveness early on.

Evaluation preparation starts with understanding the impact potential of your communication and marketing strategy. Ask yourself what outcomes you are hoping to achieve and how you can measure success – if your goal is to increase donations, measure the amount of money raised before, during (regularly) and after the implementation of your strategy.

Early evaluation allows charities to determine the impact potential of their communication strategy. By evaluating the process early, they can identify any areas of weakness and adjust their approach before it's too late. This can save time and resources in the long run and also help charities achieve their goals more efficiently. The 'bad news' is there will always be tweaks to be made to improve your marketing's role, but I suppose the 'good news' is by having this in front of mind that we can always tweak and improve, we are more likely to achieve our goals.

Regularly assessing the effectiveness of the strategy and keeping your team and community informed about the evaluation process, will help build trust, accountability and ensure everyone is working towards the same goals.

An elevator pitch can be a useful tool for obtaining buy-in and approval from leadership or team members. This is a concise and persuasive message summarising your communication strategy and why it's important. By preparing this pitch early on, you can get the buy-in you need to move forward with your strategy and make sure all concerned are on board with the plan.

One way to evaluate the impact potential of a communication strategy is by conducting a pilot test, trialling it on a small scale before implementing it on a larger scale. This allows charities to identify potential issues and make adjustments before rolling out the strategy to a broader audience. For example, a charity might test a new social media campaign on a small group of followers to see how they respond, before launching it to their entire social media audience.

To evaluate the effectiveness of a communication strategy, establish clear goals and track progress towards meeting them. You can study metrics like website traffic, social media engagement, or donations. By setting measurable goals and regularly monitoring progress, charities can identify what's working and what's not, and fine tune the strategy as needed.

Once you have established your evaluation goals and plan, it is important to incorporate feedback throughout the process. This can involve gathering feedback from stakeholders, monitoring social media and other channels for comments, or conducting surveys. Listen to suggestions and modify your strategy accordingly if appropriate. This will guarantee that your strategy remains effectively attuned to the needs of your audience. Also make sure that your communication and marketing strategy remains aligned with the core values and goals of your organisation, so that your efforts are consistent with your overall mission and vision.

There are many tools and resources available to help with evaluation preparation, including online surveys; data tracking and analysis tools; and consultation with communication and marketing professionals. Explore all available options and choose those most suited to your organisation's needs and resources.

Remember that evaluation is an ongoing process. Regular revisions should be made to ensure that your strategy remains effective and relevant. This can involve setting regular meetings with stakeholders, reviewing analytics and feedback data, and conducting periodic audits of your overall communication and marketing strategy.

Impact Potential of Marketing Ideas

Impact potential refers to the likelihood of your communication efforts creating a positive and lasting change in your target audience or broader community. Understanding your impact potential is important for several reasons. Firstly, it allows you to set realistic goals for your communication strategy and identify areas where improvements can be made. It also helps you to allocate resources and budget more effectively, ensuring that your communication efforts are targeted and impactful.

Furthermore, understanding your impact potential can help you to build credibility and support for your charity among donors, partners, and other stakeholders. By demonstrating the positive impact of your communication efforts, you can build trust and legitimacy, helping to attract new supporters and advocates for your cause.

Calculating impact potential requires a thorough understanding of your target audience, their needs and expectations, as well as the broader social, cultural, and political context in which your charity operates. It involves setting clear and measurable objectives for your communication strategy and identifying the metrics that will be used to evaluate its effectiveness.

One way to calculate impact potential is to conduct a pre and post campaign survey of your target audience to determine the extent to which your communication strategy has influenced their knowledge, attitudes, and behaviours. This could include asking questions such as:

- Have you heard of our charity before?
- Did our marketing provide you with new information?

- Did our marketing change your opinion or perception of our charity?
- Did our marketing inspire you to take action, such as volunteering or making a donation?

By analysing the survey results, you can gauge the impact potential of your communication strategy and identify areas where improvements can be made.

Another method is to track key performance indicators (KPIs) such as website traffic, social media engagement, and email open rates. By setting specific KPIs for your communication strategy, you can measure the success of your efforts and adjust your approach as needed.

Keeping Your Community Involved

When it comes to developing a new marketing and communications strategy, it's easy to get caught up in the planning and implementation stages. But it's important to remember that effective communication isn't just about the external audience – it's also about keeping your internal team and community informed and engaged throughout the process.

Why is this important? For starters, your team is the backbone of your organisation. They are the ones who will be executing your marketing and communications strategy, or advocating for it to be funded, and they need to understand the rationale behind it. Keeping your team informed about changes and updates will help with 'buy-in' and motivation. Additionally, your community is made up of stakeholders who are invested in your organisation's mission and success. These individuals may include donors, volunteers, or even the general public. By keeping them informed about your marketing and communications strategy, you can help build trust and transparency, which can in turn lead to greater support for your organisation.

So how can charities keep their teams and community informed during a new marketing and communications strategy? One important step is to involve them in the planning process from the beginning. This might be through holding brainstorming sessions or focus groups to get their input and ideas regarding the proposed strategy. By involving them from the outset, you will foster in them a feeling that their views are valued and they will become more invested in working towards success.

Another key option is to provide regular updates and communication about the strategy as it progresses, such as through regular team meetings or email updates to stakeholders. By keeping everyone informed about the progress of the strategy, you can make sure that all are on the same page and that there are no surprises when it comes to implementation. A time friendly alternative is hosting a series of 'drop by' events or webinars, that are open to the charity and are recorded for future reference.

Finally, it's important to be transparent and honest about any challenges or setbacks that may arise during the implementation. By being upfront about any issues, you can help build trust and credibility with your team and community, and demonstrate that you are committed to collaboration and open communication. And honestly, there will be things your marketing strategy hasn't considered yet that your team or supporters can bring to your attention before you start publishing messages for a larger audience.

Create the Pitch for Your Strategy

When it comes to pitching a new marketing idea or strategy for your charity, having a well-crafted elevator pitch can make all the difference. An elevator pitch is a brief, persuasive speech that you can use to spark interest in your idea and secure buy-in from your team or leadership. Here are some tips on creating a winning elevator pitch for your charity communication and marketing strategies.

Firstly, start by identifying the key message you want to convey. What is the main idea you want to communicate? Make sure it's clear, concise and compelling. Keep it short and to the point, as you want to make sure you can deliver it in 30 seconds or less.

Next, think about the problem you're trying to solve. What is the issue your charity is facing, and how will your idea help solve it? Be specific and provide data or evidence to back up your claims.

Now, consider your target audience. Who are you trying to convince? Your pitch should be tailored to your audience, highlighting the benefits that are most relevant to them.

Once you have the basic structure of your pitch, it's time to add some personality and passion. Remember, you're not just selling an idea – you're selling yourself as someone who is committed to making a difference. Use powerful language and imagery to create an emotional connection with your audience.

When it comes to pitching to leadership, be sure to frame your idea in terms of how it will benefit the organisation as a whole. Focus on how your idea aligns with the mission and values, and emphasise the positive impact it will have on the organisation's reputation and effectiveness.

Finally, practise your pitch until it feels natural and confident. This will not only help you deliver it more effectively, but also allow you to adapt it to different situations and audiences.

Never forget the importance of securing buy-in from your team. After all, they're the ones who will be responsible for implementing your idea. Be sure to involve them in the planning process and listen to their feedback. This will not only make them feel valued and invested in the project, but also help you identify any potential issues or roadblocks.

Summary

Effective marketing strategies are crucial for charities to reach their goals and achieve their missions. However, it's not enough to create and implement a plan; it's equally important to evaluate its effectiveness and potential for positive impact early on.

To this end, establish clear goals and track progress towards meeting them, by studying metrics like website traffic, social media engagement or donations. By setting measurable goals and regularly monitoring progress, you can identify what's working and what's not, and fine tune the strategy as needed.

Understanding the impact potential of your communications strategy is critical to achieving your goals. It helps you to allocate resources and budget more effectively, ensuring that your communication efforts are targeted and impactful.

Remember that effective communication isn't just about the external audience – it's also about keeping your internal team and community informed and engaged throughout the process. Your team is the backbone of your organisation. They are the ones who will be executing your marketing and communications strategy, and they need to understand the rationale behind it. Keeping your team informed about changes and updates will help with 'buy-in' and motivation.

Additionally, by keeping your community informed about your marketing and communications strategy, you will help build trust and transparency, leading in turn to greater support.

CREATIVITY'S ROLE IN CHARITY MARKETING

Is Your Marketing Creative?

When it comes to marketing, creativity is vital. Being able to think outside the box and come up with innovative solutions that stand out from the competition is essential. Creativity is especially important in campaigns, content creation and design. The good news - we can foster creativity to avoid the obvious, the boring, the underwhelming.

The first step in creating an effective creative campaign is to identify your target audience and understand their wants and needs. Once you know what they are looking for, you can create a strategy to meet those needs. This could be anything from using humour or storytelling in your messaging to highlighting customer successes or giving away special offers.

Then it's time to bring your ideas to life. This could involve working with designers to create visuals that draw attention to your message, or writing content that resonates with your audience. The most important thing is to ensure you stay true to your brand identity while also coming up with fresh and interesting ideas that will capture the attention of your target market.

Throw your values print out in clear view while you work through this section.

Lastly, you need to ensure you measure your campaign's success. Evaluating the results of each creative project will help you identify which elements were successful and which ones weren't as successful, so that you can adjust your approach for future projects.

By combining research, strategy, and creativity, you can create powerful campaigns that will get noticed and make a lasting impression on your target audience.

Creativity is an essential skill for success in the modern world. It is not only the ability to be imaginative and come up with unique ideas, but also to research and evaluate them. The challenge lies in not getting stuck in safe or boring ideas that merely meet a certain criteria, but instead pushing ourselves to stretch and explore our creative boundaries.

It is the process of engaging with existing ideas, theories, and concepts and coming up with something entirely new. Creativity can manifest itself in various forms – not just limited to art and design. It involves pushing boundaries, challenging assumptions, and breaking the rules – all in pursuit of a new and better solution.

Creativity is essential for problem-solving, innovation and progress. It enables you to explore original ideas and challenge existing norms. It also helps you stay ahead of the competition by being able to create something that is memorable and will set you apart from everyone else.

The ability to be creative helps to generate new and exciting ideas that can help you reach your goals. Whether it's coming up with a clever marketing strategy or a fresh approach to product design, creativity is essential to stand out and gain an edge in any field.

When faced with a seemingly insurmountable obstacle, creative thinking can inspire innovative solutions that might otherwise not be considered, enabling you to take advantage of opportunities others may have overlooked or missed completely. This is especially important for opening up new markets or expanding into existing ones.

Creativity helps develop new products, services, and processes which can have a significant impact on a charity's bottom line. By thinking imaginatively, a charity can unlock its true potential and ensure it remains competitive in a constantly changing environment. In short, creativity is an invaluable tool for any person or organisation looking to remain competitive and achieve success. By harnessing the creative potential within yourself and your team, you can create unique solutions to problems, develop new products and services and come up with innovative ways to succeed.

Applying creative thinking to marketing ideas can help uncover new insights, draw connections between seemingly disparate ideas and unlock solutions. Creative research can also help uncover a deeper understanding of the underlying issues that need to be addressed to move forward with a project. It allows you to look beyond the surface-level details and truly get to the heart of the problem.

There are several ways to apply creativity to marketing ideas. One effective technique is brainstorming. Brainstorming involves writing down whatever ideas come to mind without judgement or censorship. This can be done alone or in a group setting, allowing for all sorts of creative connections to be made. Another helpful technique is mind mapping. Mind mapping is a visual representation of ideas that encourages different patterns of thought.

Using creativity can also be done through curiosity and experimentation. Asking 'what if' questions can open up possibilities that would otherwise remain unseen. It also helps to be open-minded and willing to explore unfamiliar terrain.

It can be tempting to take the easy route and stick with what you know or what has been done. But while it may seem like a safe bet to stay within familiar boundaries, taking risks and experimenting with new concepts often yields the most rewarding results.
Safe or boring ideas are usually those that have been tried and tested, but no longer work effectively in today's market. Sticking with these familiar strategies can lead to stagnation and lack of progress. Additionally, a lack of originality can

lead to your ideas getting lost in a sea of similar-sounding content.

In order to stand out from the crowd, it's important to be adventurous, or at least not as risk averse (we'll talk about this later too). This means pushing yourself to explore different concepts, testing out new theories and taking risks with new ideas to ensure your content is fresh and relevant to current trends. By trying something different or using a unique approach, you can develop an interesting and engaging idea that will capture the attention of your target audience. When you take the time to explore innovative ideas, you can learn how to use various tools and techniques to become more successful in your research and creative endeavours.

The Creative Framework

You can be a creative charity no matter what your cause, the size of your organisation, or your collaborator base demographics. These details only inform the way you execute the creativity framework, not whether you can.

Before exploring the 'why' and 'how' behind each part of the creativity framework, it may be helpful to look at the ten core inspiration principles all creative charities share. Hopefully, you'll recognise most of these in your organisation. If not, use them as a jumping off point to discuss with your team how you can prioritise these principles today. With them at the core of everything you do as an organisation, both internally and externally, the creativity framework will feel like second nature.

Build Relationships with all Collaborators / Donors
The first principle of creative charities is building relationships with all of their collaborators, not just some. When a creative charity takes the time to map the collaborator journey, craft personalised messaging around each, and build the infrastructure to engage at the right time with each person, they signal to every person that they are a critical part of the organisation's mission. It doesn't matter if someone gives $100 or $1,000, no act of generosity is ignored. It might seem like building a creative relationship with all collaborators is impossible, but consider what strong relationships require – open marketing, personalised responses to signals and support of the other person's passions. You're already doing these things to cultivate lasting relationships with a small subset of collaborators. Now, you have to democratise those strategies and expand them to your entire collaborator base using resources, data and software tools available to you in today's

hyper-connected world. With creative and powerful tools like marketing automation, your team will always have a powerful way to engage with your collaborators.

Embrace Innovation and Always Looking to Improve

There's a phrase you might have heard before: 'You don't get fired for choosing IBM'. In short, it means that people tend to make the safe choice to avoid putting their own success on the line. They'd rather maintain the status quo than risk failure. In a vacuum, this might be the right approach. But collaborators do not exist in a vacuum. They're benefiting from the innovation, experimentation and failure of every brand they know. By trying to avoid failing in campaigns or projects, you're actually failing collaborators. Innovation and experimentation are the cornerstones of success.

Responsive charities are constantly innovating, experimenting and adapting their processes.
They try new things. They embrace new ideas. And they keep on improving. We are well into the 21st century. Technology is ubiquitous. The software and platforms needed to manage your data and automate your processes are available to you now. The small investment required up front can result

in exponential growth and better collaborator relationships, more than validating the purchase.

But you have to embrace the technology and processes whole-heartedly. Teach your coworkers that setbacks are an opportunity to learn and shouldn't be feared. Encourage smart, creative brainstorming based on the data you collect from your collaborators. Resist the urge to default to what's comfortable, especially when it compromises your collaborators' experience of the cause. Try again. Try something new. Evaluate failure and adopt a new approach. The more flexible and adaptable you are to change, the more exponential your growth will be.

Additionally, know that the severity of failure is drastically reduced when you use the creativity framework because you are connecting to and gaining new insights from your collaborators at all times. Every time you send an email, earn a social share or make a phone call, you're collecting data and responding to it. By constantly analysing this data, every idea you pitch will be based on facts and insights from real collaborators. Yes, you might fail sometimes, but if you're open and communicative with your collaborator base, you'll have a strong enough relationship to bounce back from any setback and move forward with greater confidence.

Outlandish decisions for the sake of shaking things up almost never do well. But original ideas born from reason and insights often do. If your collaborators trust your intention, then even if your experiments seem unconventional, they will see your vision – and believe in it.

Focus on Earning Trust

Every relationship thrives on trust and accountability. We all want to know the people we are supporting will do what they say and act in the ways we expect. Unfortunately, some charities have taken advantage of collaborators' trust over the years by mismanaging funds and making poor decisions. Some organisations have recovered from those missteps, some have not. Likely, you won't need to plan for the biggest blunders. But, you aren't immune to small mistakes or incorrect assessments and judgements. None of us are. The only way to transform those mistakes into learning opportunities rather than letting them ruin all credibility, is to work every day to earn the trust of all your collaborators.

Own the mistakes that occur through the process. Instead of hiding from these failures, communicate what went wrong with your collaborators and share how your charity is taking steps to avoid it happening again in the future. You'd be surprised what the accountability will do for your relationship.

Understand Generosity is Social and Individual
Through social media, peer-to-peer fundraising, local events, church groups etc, you can link into your collaborators' existing communities and extend an invitation for them to join yours. Through listening to what they have to say, you'll be able to identify exactly the right time to suggest new generosity opportunities for collaborators. Perhaps you'll see an opening to highlight a collaborator and their story through a series of blog posts, social media videos or newsletters. Or you might uncover an opportunity to suggest a specific group of collaborators host events that bring their friends into your charity community.

When collaborators have the chance to signal their participation, they boost their own social currency, feel more connected to your cause and more loyal to your future initiatives. You can also build a new program or community around your cause by seeking out interested collaborators and creating opportunities for them to connect with each other and your organisation.

Responsive charities take themselves out of the spotlightandhighlightthecauseandthecollaborator instead. Shift your focus to be community-driven. Create content that collaborators can share with their social circles. Seek communities that have formed around the cause or go out and build those communities yourself.

Create Good by Breaking Down Silos

In a world of shared information and multi-device connections, controlling how collaborators come to and experience your charity is impossible. They'll hear about you from friends, do their own research online, and see multiple marketings from you before you even know their name. To ensure quality and consistency for all collaborators, your internal teams must collaborate more. Silos between programs, fundraising and marketing departments no longer serve your organisation, collaborators or beneficiaries.

The more crossover between teams and collaborators, the more creative your organisation can be. Whether someone works for the organisation, donates, volunteers, or is a beneficiary of the organisation, they all have a stake and interest in the cause. Your job is to connect these people, bring them together and motivate them towards that common goal. This also means bridging the gap between the collaborators and the beneficiaries.

There are plenty of ways you can do this. Maybe you host a lecture by the researcher your charity supports, so collaborators have the chance to listen to and ask questions of the beneficiary directly. You can also host volunteer opportunities, send updates from the child or animal the collaborator is sponsoring, or even organise webinars and digital Q&As that connect field workers with collaborators. With modern technology there's no longer an excuse for keeping collaborators at an arm's length from your impact.

You can close the loop even further and let members of your organisation share their personal stories of connection to the cause. Everyone wants the same thing – to make a positive impact on the world. All you have to do is give them the opportunity for collaboration towards that common goal.

Continuously Adapt to New Behaviours

Creativity is an ongoing process with no finish line. You have to get comfortable with the idea that you'll never be done. Commit yourself to adapting to new behaviours, experimenting and innovating, over and over again. If you adopt the creativity framework, you have to keep alert to fighting stagnation. You can't default to repeating that success over and over again. True creative charities keep changing, innovating and adjusting. They are always looking to the future. As you well know, technology is changing at an exponential rate. If you're not prepared for the changes coming five, ten or fifteen years down the line, you'll fall further and further behind.

Charities are facing today's generosity crisis because they reacted to change slowly, instead of preparing for it early. The only solution is to dedicate yourself to change. If something is working, look for ways to build on it. If it stops working, come up with a new plan. If it's a wonderful success, identify how to expand it to reach more collaborators. This doesn't mean making drastic changes just for the sake of being innovative. Organisations still need to be incredibly thoughtful about the changes they make. Take a creative view. Listen to your collaborators, connect with them, and then continually make adjustments informed by what you learn.

Say Thank You Three Times for Every Ask of Generosity

The funniest moment in a new parent's life is when your child begins mimicking your behaviour.

Whether it's waving back when you say hello or repeating that curse word you hoped they wouldn't hear, humans mirror behaviour from a very early age. That mirroring doesn't stop as we age. In fact, though we become more aware of how others influence our behaviours and actions, that doesn't stop their influence from being effective. Knowing this, creative charities template the same generous behaviour they're asking for from their collaborators.

There's a saying: 'Generosity begets generosity'. This means giving back to your collaborators even more than they give to you – prioritising your relationship over their money. Unfortunately, many charities treat their collaborators like an ATM, but those same organisations are finding that the account is dwindling. Responsive organisations, however, work to provide significant experiences before collaborators give. Never lose sight of the sacrifices your supporters are making with their time and money. Put your gratitude to them first and engage with them without asking for money. Once you begin engaging with them in this way, you'll be able to give them something valuable in return – an emotional experience.

To do this at scale for all your collaborators, you can automate these engagements, creating emails and workflows that trigger automatically to share this messaging with your audience. You don't have to handwrite 1,000 notes every day, but you do have to dedicate yourself to giving more than you are asking if you want the relationship to grow. Remember, you must continuously evaluate, innovate and adjust those processes. The flows may be automated, but the content and thought you put into them should always be considerate and personalised.

Value Motivational Insights over Behavioural Ones

Marketing is a series of signals and responses. Sometimes these signals are verbal, but sometimes they're physical, behavioural, or even unconscious. For example, let's say you go to coffee with a friend and catch up on their life. She begins to tell you about the stress at her job, and you notice from physical signals that she's tired and feeling defeated. Maybe there are circles under her eyes or her shoulders are slumping. She orders a coffee but doesn't even drink it. All of these are signals, and once you pick up on them, you know to respond with comforting words, maybe a hug or an offer to help. Throughout this seemingly simple exchange, you've displayed a level of emotional intelligence that informed your actions.

Organisations require a strong level of emotional intelligence to be creative. Knowing how to listen to collaborator signals, form connections, and make informed suggestions all require a mature, analytical ability. So many charities get caught up with a single behavioural signal – 'Did they donate or not'? – that they fail to listen to all the other signals collaborators are giving. Their analysis is rooted only in dollar amounts and number of clicks, ignoring everything else. Responsive charities, however, seek out the motivation behind the behaviour first. They don't value what someone is doing as much as why they're doing it.

For example, let's say you send your collaborators a video about a new well your team is building. You aren't interested in how many collaborators watched the video, but why some clicked play and others didn't. What motivated those who watched and what disengaged those who didn't? Knowing why someone is moved to learn about or support a certain cause is more important than the mere fact that they're donating. Once you know their why, you can tailor all future interactions to them and make appropriate suggestions based on a comprehensive collaborator journey.

Believe Generosity is not Transactional

People give for many reasons. They give out of grief, anger, frustration, love and compassion – the list goes on. The disconnect between a collaborator and a charity begins when the organisation focuses on the act of giving, rather than the human heart at its centre. Don't forget the emotion that sits at the heart of generosity. Responsive charities need to embrace a shift in mindset that moves away from treating generosity as a transaction and instead recognises it for the sacrifice it is.

Donors don't get anything in return for their generosity except for a reminder that they did some good. That isn't a substantial enough reason on its own to encourage lifelong generosity in the face of being treated as an ATM. Whether it's as little as $10 or as monumental as $1 million, the donation is still meaningful to that person. You have to do whatever you can, whenever you can, to create a relationship with your donors and recognise their generosity. Your cause means a lot to them, and you are their biggest, often only, connection to a purpose they care about. Don't take that responsibility lightly.

Amount Doesn't Reflect Passion

Who cares the most about your cause – you or your collaborator? You may believe that, because you are behind the wheel of a charity dedicated to a particular cause, you represent the highest level of concern for it. You sacrifice your time, effort, maybe even finances to the cause, but that does not mean you have more passion for it than your collaborators.

You can't take a tone of superiority in fundraising or assume that the strength of the connection your collaborator has is demonstrated in the amount donated. Someone who is only able to donate $5 a month may be perceived as a low-interest supporter, but until you get to know them you won't have a true grasp of their level of concern. That $5 monthly donor may have lost a friend to cancer, and now seeks to scrape by whatever they can to donate to its research. You won't know their level of passion until you connect with them personally. No matter how much someone donates, at the end of the day every collaborator is making a sacrifice, and they deserve to be honoured for it. Donors deserve a democratic experience. You shouldn't treat collaborators differently based on the amount they give, and you can't relate the amount to a perceived level of concern. Here's a challenge that I encourage you to take at your charity. What would change about your fundraising strategy if you assumed that every collaborator cares more about the cause than you do?

Equipped with the knowledge of these inspiration principles, your charity should strive to be creative as an organisation. It's important to remember that creativity is often born out of trial and error. Don't be afraid to experiment and test ideas; sometimes you have to try things before you can discover what works best. Give yourself time and space away from the hustle and bustle of everyday life and allow yourself time to think and reflect.

By being creative in your research and idea generation, you can unlock innovative solutions to problems that will take your projects to the next level. It's a process that requires dedication, but with a bit of practice, you'll soon find yourself producing more effective outcomes than ever before.

Creativity can be Fostered

Creativity is a key ingredient in any successful marketing and communication strategy, and this is especially true for charities. By thinking inventively and taking risks, charities can capture the attention and hearts of their audience and drive engagement and support for their cause.

But how do you go about fostering creativity? Here are a few steps you can take to help you get started:

- Take a break. Step away from your task and give yourself some space to think. This can help you see your task from a new perspective and spark new ideas.
- Ask yourself or colleagues questions about the task to uncover potential ideas or paths forward, using 'out of the box' questions that challenge traditional ways of thinking.
- Collaboration. Brainstorming with a team or partner can help to stimulate creative thought and reveal different perspectives towards the same problem.
- Be open to serendipity. Don't be afraid to take a chance and explore something improbable. A different approach may lead to unique and original ideas that could revolutionise your work. However, it's important to evaluate and adjust your strategy as needed to ensure that your efforts are having the desired impact.
- Engage in play. Experiment and play around with different ideas – don't be afraid to make mistakes. By allowing yourself to explore freely, you'll open yourself up to a world of possibility that could bring you amazing results.

By following these steps, you'll be able to foster creative thinking and come up with fresh, new ideas. With some hard work, dedication, and a bit of luck, you'll be able to create something truly special!

When it comes to generating new ideas, it's important to ask the right questions. Questions can help push you out of a rut and force you to think imaginatively. Here are some questions to get the creative juices flowing:

- What would this look like if I did it differently?
- How can I make this idea more unique or unusual?
- Who could I collaborate with to make this idea even better?
- What results am I trying to achieve?
- Are there any unconventional methods that could help me reach my goals?
- What could I do to make this concept stand out from the crowd?
- How can I use my strengths to create something unique?
- Is there any way to combine two different ideas into one?
- What unexpected uses could this have?
- Are there any problems that need solving in this field?

Drawing inspiration from your mission can help you develop ideas that are not only creative but also aligned with your organisation's values. Your charity's mission is at the heart of everything you do, so use it as a source of inspiration for your marketing and communication ideas. Think about how you can bring your mission to life in a way that will resonate with your audience and drive engagement.

Ultimately, creativity and focus are essential for charities looking to boost their communication and marketing ideas. By thinking imaginatively, drawing inspiration from their mission, collaborating with their team and stakeholders, using storytelling, and taking risks, charities can develop impactful and successful marketing campaigns that drive engagement and support for their cause.

Thinking Beyond the Obvious

Playing it safe with humdrum and generic marketing campaigns is a surefire way to blend in with the crowd and fail to stand out from the competition. Charities have a unique opportunity to connect with their audience on an emotional level and inspire them to take action, but this requires a bold and original approach.

By taking risks and trying something new, charities can capture attention and generate excitement around their cause. A marketing campaign that is fresh and engaging is much more likely to capture the hearts and minds of the audience than one that is dull and predictable.

Moreover, in today's dynamic, fast-paced and crowded digital world, it is more important than ever to grab the attention of potential supporters and donors. With so many messages bombarding people every day, it can be difficult to cut through the noise and be noticed. By being adventurous, charities can make a memorable impression and create a lasting impact.

Finally, playing it safe with common and boring marketing campaigns can also lead to a lack of differentiation among charities. With so many organisations competing for attention and funding, it is crucial to stand out and differentiate oneself from the rest. By being creative and taking risks, charities can establish a unique identity and build a loyal following of supporters. Here are some strategies you can take to make sure your customers don't die of boredom with your next marketing campaign:

- Tap into pop culture. Use current trends, memes, or popular social media challenges as inspiration for your campaigns. This will make your content feel fresh and relevant, and it can help you reach a wider audience.

• Use humour. This can be a great way to engage with your audience and make your content more shareable. Be careful to avoid being offensive or insensitive.

• Make it interactive! Create games, quizzes, or other interactive content that encourages your audience to engage with your brand. This can be a great way to build a community around your cause and drive engagement.

• Get artistic and use visuals. Visual content like videos, images, or infographics can be more engaging than text alone. Use high-quality visuals that are on-brand and relevant to your cause.

• User-generated content. Encourage your supporters to create and share their own content related to your cause, such as photos, videos, or personal stories. Sharing user-generated content can help build a sense of community and showcase the impact of your work.

• Create a hashtag. A catchy hashtag can be a great way to encourage your audience to engage with your brand and share their own content related to your cause. Make sure to use a unique hashtag that is easy to remember and relevant to your brand.

- Tell personal stories about the charity and the people it supports. These can be a powerful way to connect with your audience and showcase the impact of your work. Use real-life examples to illustrate the impact of your cause and inspire support.
- Finally, use influencer marketing. Partner with stakeholders with an audience who are aligned with your cause to help amplify your message and reach a wider audience. Make sure to choose influencers who are authentic and genuine in their support of your cause.

Brand Storytelling

Brand storytelling is an effective way for charities to connect with their audience and build recognition. Stories have the ability to connect with people on an emotional level, which can help to drive action and inspire support for your cause. Use storytelling in your marketing and communication to showcase the impact of your work and engage with your audience in a meaningful way.

By crafting a narrative that resonates with your audience, you can create an emotional connection that drives engagement and support for your cause. Here are some different opportunities for brand storytelling that you and your charity can explore:

- *Origin story:* Your charity's origin story is a powerful tool for brand storytelling. It allows you to share your mission and values in a compelling way, while also showcasing the impact that your organisation has had on the community.
- *Success stories:* Sharing these is an effective way to demonstrate the impact of your work and inspire support for your cause. By highlighting the stories of individuals or communities that your organisation has helped, you can connect with your audience on an emotional level and showcase the positive impact of your work.
- *Behind-the-scenes:* Giving your audience a behind-the-scenes look at your organisation can help to humanise your brand and build trust with your audience. By showcasing the people and processes behind your organisation, you can give your audience a better understanding of your mission and values.
- *Collaborations:* Collaborating with other organisations or individuals can provide unique opportunities for brand storytelling. By working with partners who share your mission and values, you can showcase the collective

impact of your work and inspire support for your cause.

• *Brand personality:* Developing a distinct brand personality can help your organisation stand out in a crowded marketplace. By infusing your marketing and communication with your organisation's unique tone, voice, and values, you can create a memorable and engaging brand experience for your audience.

• *Brand heritage:* If your organisation has a long history, you can leverage that heritage as a tool for brand storytelling. By sharing stories and artefacts from your organisation's past, you can connect with your audience on an emotional level and demonstrate the enduring impact of your work.

• *User-generated content:* User-generated content is a powerful tool for brand storytelling. By encouraging your audience to share their own stories and experiences related to your cause, you can create a sense of community and engagement around your brand.

• *Social media:* Social media provides unique opportunities for brand storytelling, from sharing user-generated content to creating engaging videos and graphics. By leveraging social media to tell your brand story, you can reach a wider audience and drive engagement for your cause.

Summary

When it comes to marketing, creativity is vital to avoid the risk of boring or underwhelming ideas and perception. Being able to think outside the box and come up with innovative solutions that stand out from the competition is essential. Creativity is especially important in campaigns, content creation and design.

All creative charities share ten inspirational principles, centred around building genuine relationships with each collaborator and donor, understanding that generosity is social and individual, and always looking for ways to improve.

Creativity can be fostered through a variety of methods, including taking time-out breaks; asking questions that force you to think imaginatively; brainstorming with a team or partner; engaging in play; and being open to serendipity.

An effective creative campaign involves identifying your target audience and creating a strategy to meet their needs. By taking risks and trying something new, charities can capture attention and generate excitement around their cause.

A marketing campaign that is fresh, original, and engaging is much more likely to capture the hearts and minds of the audience than one that is dull and predictable. This could involve using humour or storytelling in your messaging to highlight successes, or giving away special offers. With some hard work, dedication and a bit of luck, you'll be able to come up with fresh, new ideas and create something truly special!

Action Guide: Creative Thinking Questions

12 seemingly ridiculous questions and prompts to use to encourage creative thinking and challenge marketing ideas and plans:

1. If your brand were an animal, what would it be, and how would it communicate with other animals? How could you apply this to your communication strategy?

2. Imagine your product or service is being launched on Mars. How would you adapt your communication ideas to effectively reach and engage the Martian population?

3. If your target audience suddenly lost the ability to read, how would you convey your key messages using only visuals or sounds?

4. What would your communication plan look like if you had an unlimited budget?

5. How could you achieve a similar impact with only 5% of YOUR CURRENT budget?

6. Imagine you're pitching your communication idea to a group of sceptical toddlers. How would you simplify and make your idea more engaging for them?

7. Imagine your product or service is the main character in a blockbuster movie. What would its storyline be, and how would you use that narrative to enhance your communication efforts?

8. How would you promote your charity if all forms of digital communication ceased to exist? What traditional or unconventional methods would you use to get your message across?

9. Your entire target audience develops a sudden, intense interest in underwater basket weaving. How could you incorporate this newfound passion into your communication strategy?

10. Imagine your brand is hosting a reality TV show. What would the show's concept be, and how could it be leveraged to amplify your communication efforts?

11. If your brand were a superhero, what would its superpowers be, and how would you use these powers to create a memorable and engaging communication campaign?

12. What would your communication strategy look like if it were designed by a famous artist (e.g., Picasso, Banksy, or Frida Kahlo)? How could you bring elements of their signature style or approach into your efforts?

Use these ridiculous questions and prompts to stimulate creative thinking and challenge your marketing ideas and plans. The goal is to push boundaries, explore unconventional solutions, and spark innovative ideas that can help your brand stand out and make a lasting impact. Remember, even the most outrageous ideas can contain nuggets of inspiration that can be adapted to fit your charity context.

TESTING YOUR MARKETING IDEAS

Charities rely on effective marketing to spread awareness and achieve their missions. With limited resources and tight budgets, they must get their messaging right upfront. That's why charities need to test-run their new marketing and marketing strategies before deploying them to the public. This allows charities to identify any flaws in their messaging or approach before it goes public. It can save time, money, and resources in the long run by avoiding costly mistakes or negative feedback. By testing and adjusting their strategy, charities can ensure that their messaging is clear, compelling and resonates with their target audience.

One key benefit of testing a new strategy is the ability to gather feedback and insights from stakeholders. This includes internal team members, board members, and external partners or customers. Soliciting feedback from different perspectives can help charities identify blind spots or areas for improvement that may have been overlooked otherwise. This feedback can also help build buy-in and support for the new strategy by involving stakeholders and making them feel heard and valued.

Testing can help charities identify the most effective channels and tactics for reaching their target audience. For example, a charity may have assumed that social media would be the most effective way to reach younger audiences. Still, testing may reveal that targeted email campaigns actually yield better results. By identifying the most effective channels and tactics, charities can optimise their resources and maximise their impact.

Another benefit of testing is the ability to measure the potential impact of the new strategy before deploying it on a larger scale. This can help charities set realistic goals and expectations, and adjust their approach as needed to achieve those goals. By measuring the potential impact, charities can also better allocate resources and budget to ensure that the strategy is effective and efficient.

Testing can take many forms, from small-scale focus groups to large-scale pilot programmes. It's important for charities to determine the appropriate testing level based on the new strategy's scope and resources. For smaller initiatives, a focus group or survey may be sufficient. For larger initiatives, a pilot programme or beta launch may be necessary to fully test and refine the strategy before launching it publicly.

In addition to testing the strategy itself, it's also important for charities to test the messaging and creative elements of their marketing. This includes headlines, visuals and calls to action. By testing these elements, charities can identify which ones resonate most with their audience and adjust accordingly. This can help increase engagement and drive action from the target audience.

Continually testing and adjusting a marketing strategy allows a charity to stay agile and adapt to changing circumstances or new information. It also helps ensure that their messaging remains relevant and effective in the ever-changing landscape of marketing and communication.

The Role of Research

Strategy, team, culture, tools and processes are all the bedrock of an effective charity, but if this bedrock lacks research, it will end up disintegrating. Research is a crucial step in developing and validating your brand. It can be time-consuming, but it is necessary to ensure success. Knowing when and how to brainstorm, set a tight time frame, involve the right people, and move on with the project, is vital. With the right tools and strategies, you can easily turn research into a powerful asset for your brand.

Research enables a thorough understanding of marketing objectives, potential risks and benefits and key stakeholders. Research is the foundation that we build upon, the starting point for strategy development and implementation. In terms of marketing idea validation, research is essential in order to determine the needs and wants of customers and other stakeholders. It helps us to understand the competitive landscape, customer preferences, and industry trends. All of this information helps us to identify areas of opportunity or risk, as well as to design initiatives that meet customer needs.

Research can also be used to identify influencers and advocates within the market who have significant influence on customer decisions. By engaging with these influencers, we can create powerful conversations about our brand and reach more people than by using traditional marketing efforts.

Research is the beginning of any successful brand validation effort, and should not be overlooked or rushed through. Taking the time to conduct thorough research is invaluable in ensuring that we are making informed decisions and optimising our chances for success. It's important to make sure everyone is on the same page and knows what their role is in the process.

Brainstorming is an important part of the research process, and is essential to finding the best path forward for your brand. It allows you to quickly generate multiple ideas and reveal different directions for exploration. It's a valuable tool to help you discover new possibilities and come up with creative solutions.

When brainstorming, it's important to set aside enough time to adequately explore different ideas. If you rush through the process, you may end up missing out on potential opportunities or finding yourself limited in terms of options. Having a solid timeline for brainstorming also allows ample opportunity for different departments or people within your organisation to provide input, while helping them stay focused and productive throughout the process.

Ensure that all relevant stakeholders are involved in the process to promote shared agreement around key messages and the direction of the brand.

Once the brainstorming process has been completed, it's important to validate your findings. Validating a successful brand is one of the most important steps in its development. This involves researching what has been done before, brainstorming ideas with key stakeholders, and examining the viability of any ideas with time-bound objectives. The research stage is important because it helps you understand the market and gain insights into the needs and expectations of your target audience, as well as determining if the ideas generated will fit with the overall goals of your brand.

A timeline for validating your brand and its associated messaging should include a schedule for the testing of certain elements, as well as the announcement of results. To ensure this process is as effective as possible, it's important to include different business areas within your organisation in the validation process.

Cross-check Ideas with Intended Outcomes

If you don't have one already, create an intended outcomes one-pager that defines your charity goals, activities, outputs, inputs, outcomes, and impact. This will serve an important role as a visual summary of your border work. This visualisation is essential to get everyone literally on the same page and is a vital cross-check with working with new marketing ideas or approaches.

The intended outcomes template is defined as a picture of how your organisation does its work – the theory and assumptions underlying the program. A template can link charity outcomes (both short and long term) with program activities or processes, and the intended outcomes.

At the end of the day, you want a visual summary that depicts what your program does and what change is expected as a result.

Your intended outcomes template could include:

- *Goals:* What do we hope to change at a broad level?
- *Inputs:* What resources will we invest as part of our work?

- *Activities:* What events, action steps, or activities will happen?
- *Outputs*: What does our work produce? (attendees,materialsdistributed,membership renewed, intake forms, events, etc.)
- *Outcomes*: What actually changed for our participants?

Example: Intended outcomes template (Youth Tutoring Program)
The example of a fictitious youth tutoring program will be used to illustrate various elements throughout this section.

The common themes are students and academic success. The five components flow from the big picture – the goal – to the measurable change expected to occur – the outcomes. The overall flow shows what is going into the program (inputs and activities), followed by what the results of the program will be (outputs and expected outcomes).

As you create your own, keep in mind all of these components should appear related:

Goal
Your goal is a broad statement of what you hope to change. It is focused on the broad strokes; it is not specific or measurable. It should also align

with your mission statement. The goal statement from the *Youth Tutoring Program* is 'To improve the academic achievement of students so they can achieve their full academic potential'. The terms 'Improve academic achievement' and 'full academic potential' address in general ways how the program is intended to help students. It is clear from this statement they are providing services to students, so there's an overall understanding of what the program does.

Examples for other program types might be:

- To help teaching artists connect with each other to enrich their teaching practice.
- To provide resources, relationships and advocacy to help end homelessness.

Inputs

Inputs refer to the resources for a program to operate, including people, space, equipment, funds, and anything or anyone else that's needed.

Example: Inputs (Youth Tutoring Program)

This fictional template includes three inputs: space for tutoring sessions, three tutors and a tutoring plan created in collaboration with schools.

Other input examples:

- Staff (FTE) to run the program.
- Partnerships.
- Materials (handouts, curriculum).
- Equipment (computers, phones).

Activities

Activities are the essential actions that make your charity go. They're what you talk about when someone asks what your program does.

Example: Activities (Youth Tutoring Program)

For the Youth Tutoring program, activities provide academic instruction at least twice a week and provide ongoing guidance to encourage school attendance and increase hours spent on schoolwork. These two activities are clearly aligned to the goal and inputs, illustrating the specifics of how the program is carried out. Here are more sample activities:

- Provide mathematics and science activities in fourth and fifth grade classrooms.
- Deliver food boxes to homeless shelters.
- Provide sight and hearing screening for people without access to quality health care.

Outputs

Outputs are the measurable evidence that your program is operating. They show the level of participation, but not necessarily what kind of difference your charity is making.

Example: Outputs (Youth Tutoring Program)

In this example the outputs are the numbers of students, tutoring sessions delivered and number of participating schools. Other example outputs include:

- Number of food boxes delivered.
- Number of patients treated.
- Number of homeless families housed.

Outcomes

Outcomes measure changes as a result of the program in terms of knowledge, skills, attitudes and/or behaviour. Outcomes are a key ingredient in the program evaluation plan.

Example: Outcomes (Youth Tutoring Program)

As a result of participating in the program, student behaviour toward attendance is expected to change. The academic achievement of students is also expected to improve. Some other sample outcome statements may be:

- To increase student interest in STEM related careers (Science, technology, engineering and mathematics).
- To improve housing stability.
- To improve health conditions for low-income residents.

Questions to Crosscheck your Marketing Idea with your Charity's Intended Outcomes:

- What is your marketing idea's goal? Is it similar to your charity's goal?
- Who is involved with delivering your idea - how will it affect inputs?
- How many people will your marketing idea reach before it affects outputs?
- What are your core activities of your marketing idea?
- What are your measurable outcomes that directly relate to the charity's outcomes?
- How will you measure progress toward those outcomes and not drift away from them?

Test, Validate, Adjust

Marketing campaigns can be a powerful tool for charities to engage with their audience, raise awareness, and generate support for their cause. However, ensuring that your marketing campaign is effective and resonates with your audience is important. This is where quick testing, validation, and adjustment strategies come into play.

First, define your metrics for success. Before launching a marketing campaign, it is essential to determine what success looks like for your organisation. Set clear and measurable goals, such as the number of donations, website visits, or social media engagement. This will help you track your progress and evaluate the effectiveness of your marketing campaign.

Next, conduct a small-scale test. Before launching your marketing campaign to a wider audience, consider conducting a small-scale test with a subset of your target audience. This can help you gauge initial reactions and identify any issues or opportunities for improvement before rolling out the campaign to a larger audience.

You May Like to Utilise A/B Testing

This involves comparing two marketing campaign versions to determine which performs better. It can include testing different headlines, images, or calls to action. By using A/B testing, you can identify what works best for your audience and make adjustments accordingly.

Gather Feedback and Insights

Feedback from your audience can provide valuable insights into what is and isn't working with your marketing campaign. Encourage your audience to provide feedback through surveys, social media, or other channels. Analyse the feedback and use it to make adjustments to your campaign.

Monitor and Adjust in Real-Time

Marketing campaigns should be monitored and adjusted in real-time based on the results and feedback. Utilise data analytics tools to track the performance of your campaign and adjust your strategy accordingly.

Incorporate User-Generated Content

User-generated content can be a powerful tool for engaging with your audience and showcasing the impact of your organisation. Encourage your audience to create and share content related to your campaign, such as photos or videos. Incorporate this content into your marketing campaign to increase engagement and authenticity.

Engage with Micro-Influencers

Micro-influencers are individuals with a smaller but highly engaged social media following. Engaging with micro-influencers can be a cost-effective way to reach a highly engaged and targeted audience. Identify micro-influencers in your space and collaborate with them to promote your marketing campaign.

Incorporating Feedback

Feedback is an essential tool for any charity to improve its marketing ideas and campaigns. Why is it so important for charities to seek and incorporate feedback into their marketing campaigns? Here are a few key reasons:

- *Improved effectiveness:* By listening to feedback and making changes based on what your audience is telling you, you can improve the effectiveness of your campaigns. This can lead to better engagement, more donations, and ultimately, greater impact.
- *Builds trust and loyalty*: When your audience sees that you're actively listening to their feedback and making changes based on their input, it can help build trust and loyalty. This can be especially important for charities, where trust is often a key factor in donors' decisions to support a cause.
- *Maintains relevancy:* The world is constantly changing, and what worked yesterday may not work tomorrow. By seeking feedback and staying attuned to your audience's needs and

preferences, you can stay relevant and adapt to changing trends and circumstances.

- *Encourages engagement*: When people feel like their voices are being heard, they're more likely to engage with your campaigns and support your cause.

Incorporating feedback into your marketing is a powerful way to improve your approach, build trust and loyalty, and stay relevant in a rapidly changing world. By listening to what your audience has to say, you can refine your approach and make sure you're delivering the right message to the right people. But how do you go about incorporating feedback into your campaigns? Here are some steps to get you started:

- *Collect and compile feedback:* The first step is to gather feedback from your audience. This can be done through surveys, focus groups, or simply monitoring social media channels for comments and mentions. Once you've collected the feedback, compile it into a clear and concise summary so that you can easily refer back to it.
- Not all feedback is created equal, and it's important to identify the most valuable and actionable insights. Look for common themes and patterns in the feedback to help identify the areas needing attention. This might

include things like messaging, tone, design, or even the channels you're using to reach your audience.

- *Create an action plan:* Once you've identified the top bits of feedback, create an action plan to address them. This might involve tweaking your messaging or design, adjusting your targeting or segmentation, or even rethinking your entire approach. Make sure your action plan is specific, measurable, and achievable, and set clear timelines and milestones for each step.
- *Test and refine:* As you implement your action plan, continue to test and refine your approach based on the feedback you receive. Use metrics like engagement rates, click-through rates, and conversion rates to measure the impact of your changes and make further adjustments as needed.

Communicate your progress: Let your audience know that you've heard their feedback and are taking steps to improve your approach. This can help build trust and engagement, and encourage further feedback in the future.

Values Check-in

Charities are responsible for upholding their values and missions in every aspect of their operations, including their marketing strategies. However, in the pursuit of creating a successful campaign, it can be easy to lose sight of the organisation's core values. This is why it is crucial for charities to check that their marketing strategy aligns with their values before launching it to the public.

One of the primary reasons why alignment with values is important is that it helps to maintain the trust of stakeholders. Charities rely on the support and donations of their stakeholders, and trust is essential in building and maintaining those relationships. When a charity's marketing campaign contradicts its values, stakeholders may question the charity's authenticity and integrity, potentially leading to a loss of support.

Moreover, a misaligned marketing strategy can be detrimental to a charity's reputation. In today's digital age, it only takes one misstep for a charity to face significant backlash on social media or other platforms. Any negative attention can undermine a charity's efforts and cause lasting damage to their reputation, which can ultimately impact their ability to achieve their mission.

To avoid these negative consequences, charities must take the time to review their marketing strategy and ensure that it aligns with their values. The first step is to define the organisation's core values and mission. These values should be the foundation of every decision made by the charity, including marketing and communications. Next, the charity should review its marketing materials and assess whether they align with its values and mission. This includes reviewing messaging, imagery, and any other marketing channels used to promote the campaign. If there are any discrepancies or misalignments, adjustments should be made before the campaign is launched.

It is also vital for charities to involve their team in this process. Every member of the team should be aware of the organisation's values and mission and understand how they apply to the marketing campaign. Team members can offer valuable insights and perspectives, which can help identify any potential misalignments or inconsistencies.

In some cases, charities may need to make difficult decisions about certain aspects of their marketing campaign that conflict with their values. For example, a charity may be tempted to use sensationalist or exploitative imagery to attract attention to their cause. However, this approach can backfire and cause significant harm to the charity's reputation. In these cases, it is essential to stay true to the organisation's values and seek alternative approaches that align with the mission.

Summary

It's important for charities to continuously test and adjust their marketing strategies. This allows them to stay agile and adapt to changing circumstances or new information. It also helps ensure that their messaging remains relevant and effective in the ever-changing landscape of marketing and communication.

Testing is an essential piece of the marketing puzzle, crucial in developing and validating your charity's brand. It can be time-consuming, but it is necessary to ensure success. In terms of brand validation, testing is essential in order to determine the needs and wants of customers and other stakeholders. It helps you understand the competitive landscape, customer preferences, and industry trends. All of this information helps to identify areas of opportunity or risk; develop effective strategies; and design marketing initiatives that are relevant, meet customer needs and differentiate your organisation from others.

The process involves brainstorming, stakeholder engagement, defining the metrics of success, incorporating feedback and ensuring your marketing strategy and values are in alignment.

A visual representation of your program can be created using a charity program overview, an impact template or a research audit. The elements of each vary slightly, enabling you to choose the most appropriate tool for summarising what your program does and what outcomes you expect.

COLLABORATION CONSIDERATION

Collaboration is a significant element of effective marketing and the ability to have your message heard above all the environmental noise. Effective collaboration requires teamwork and trust between all parties involved. There are a few critical elements to consider when incorporating collaboration into your marketing mix.

When collaborating on a marketing project, the team should work together to identify objectives, create timelines, and assign roles and responsibilities. Clear communication is essential to ensure that everyone understands their part to play and that no detail is overlooked.

Effective collaboration can help you identify potential risks or problems that may arise during the project. By working together, team members can come up with solutions to any issues that may arise before they become a problem. This allows for quick problem-solving and can prevent delays in execution. Team members should also provide feedback throughout the process. This will help ensure that everyone is on the same page and allow for creative solutions to be proposed. Open dialogue and the ability to compromise are both necessary in developing an effective marketing strategy.

Once the collaboration process is completed, all parties should be aware of the final expectations and results. This will allow everyone to move forward in executing the plan with a clear understanding of their roles and the goals set.

The benefits of effective collaboration go beyond just marketing ideas. It promotes open communication and problem-solving skills which can help team members work together more efficiently in any situation to achieve success.

Potential and Initiation

Effective marketing is essential for the success of any charity organisation, and collaborating with the right partners can take your marketing strategy to the next level. But how can charities find the right marketing collaboration opportunities? Identifying potential collaborators can be a daunting task, but there are some key steps you can take to make the process easier.

Firstly, consider who in your network has a similar mission or audience to yours. Are there other organisations that share your values and are working towards a similar goal? These organisations could be valuable collaborators, as you can work together to amplify each other's message and reach a wider audience.

Another option is to look for individuals or organisations with a large social media following or strong influence in your sector. Micro-influencers, for example, may have a smaller following than celebrity influencers, but their audience is often more engaged and targeted to your cause. Collaborating with micro-influencers can help you reach new and relevant audiences.

The first step is identifying potential collaborators who share your organisation's values and mission. Look for organisations and individuals who are working in the same space and have similar goals. Consider local businesses, other charities, community groups, and even government agencies.

Once you have identified potential collaborators, it's essential to carefully time your marketing approach in order to make it easy for them to support your strategy. Are there any events, milestones or campaigns coming up that would be relevant to both your causes? Are there crossovers in your strategies? Consider reaching out to organisations or individuals who are involved in these events or campaigns to start the conversation and pitch your ideas.

It's important to be clear about what you're asking for and what you can offer in return. Make sure your marketing strategy aligns with the other party's interests and priorities. Focus on building long term relationships rather than one-off collaborations.

Make it Easy for Stakeholders

Timing your marketing strategy is critical to ensuring that your message is heard by your target audience at the right time. Whether you are promoting an event, fundraising campaign or advocacy initiative, it's important to choose the right moment to engage with your audience.
Consider the key dates and events that may impact your marketing strategy. Are there any holidays, anniversaries, or awareness days that are relevant to your cause? Timing your marketing around these

events can help increase visibility and engagement with your target audience. Timing can also be influenced by external factors, such as breaking news or trends on social media.

Once you have identified the timing for your marketing strategy, it's important to make it easy for stakeholders to support your approach. You may create a simple promotional pack that provides key messages, images, and social media posts that stakeholders can easily share with their networks. This pack could be emailed to key stakeholders, posted on your website, or shared on social media. You can also create branded merchandise or materials that can be distributed to supporters at events or in your community.

Another way to make it easy for stakeholders to support your approach is to leverage the power of micro-influencers. Consider partnering with local influencers or advocates who are passionate about your cause and have a strong following in your community.

It's also important to communicate to stakeholders the impact of their support. Share success stories, statistics and updates on how their involvement is making a difference. This can be done through regular email updates, social media posts, or face to face meetings. By showing the importance and effect of their support, you can increase engagement and build stronger relationships.

In summary, timing your marketing strategy and making it easy for stakeholders to support your approach are fundamental components of a successful marketing campaign for charities. So, take the time to plan and execute a well-timed marketing strategy and watch your organisation grow and succeed.

Micro-influencers

In today's digital age, social media has become a powerful tool for charities to reach out to their audience and raise awareness of their cause. However, with so much content out there, it can be challenging for charities to have their message heard. This is where micro-influencers come in.

Micro-influencers are individuals with a relatively small but highly engaged following on social media. They are seen as more authentic and relatable than celebrities or macro-influencers, and as such, can be an effective way for charities to reach a wider audience.

One of the benefits of working with micro-influencers is that they often have a niche audience that aligns with the charity's target demographic. This can make it easier for the charity to reach people who are interested in their cause and more likely to engage with their content.

To find the right micro-influencers, charities can use social media platforms like Instagram and Twitter to search for individuals who are already engaging with their cause. A good influencer will be passionate about the charity's cause and will have a genuine interest in promoting it to their followers. On the other hand, a bad influencer may be seen as disingenuous and could damage the charity's reputation.

Once the right micro-influencers have been identified, it's important to establish clear expectations and guidelines for the partnership. This may include the frequency and type of content to be posted, the tone and messaging, and any specific hashtags or calls to action.

It's also important to measure the success of the partnership. Charities can use analytics tools on social media platforms to track engagement and reach, and evaluate the impact of the micro-influencer campaign.

To make it easy for micro-influencers to promote your charity, you can create a simple promo pack that includes information about the charity's mission and goals, as well as social media graphics, images, and videos that the influencers can use in their posts.

It's important to remember that micro-influencers are not a silver bullet solution for your charity's marketing efforts. They should be viewed as part of a larger, integrated marketing strategy that includes a range of marketing channels and tactics. With the right approach, working with micro-influencers can be a powerful tool for charities to raise awareness and expand support for their cause.

Charity Connection

Sometimes a good option for your collaborative event is to find another organisation that is similar in scope to yours and thinking along the same lines. This allows you to pool the resources that you have in order to make a bigger and better event that more people would be interested in. There are many ways to go about finding charity organisations who are also looking to hold collaborative events.

While searching, approach it as if you were implementing an advertising plan yourself. Check social media, online postings, in store postings and community message boards for all types of information regarding organisations. If an organisation already has an event in place, talk with them about potential collaborations. More than likely, the idea of pooling together collaborators and resources will be very appealing. Just make sure your goals are not in totally different directions – this would cause confusion among the collaborators and community members.

Two teams working together brings the ability to pool sponsor resources, manpower and ease time management pressures, while successfully organising a much bigger event with mutual benefits.

Some organisations will have networking connections in place, where you'll be able to find new participants and donors of your own. The same works for the company that is choosing to collaborate with you; likely they have this very same idea in mind. It doesn't take away from anybody's donors and it's not a competition, because all the money raised is going towards very important causes. Always remember this if you feel a competitive hesitancy during this part of the process.

When you pool your resources, this means that everything will be shared. Means for advertising the event will increase; businesses will be more encouraged to become a part of the event and the community as a whole will want to become a part of something which is bound to be huge. Volunteers will also be encouraged to work harder knowing they have a larger team and will be able to draw more donations. Coming together with another organisation is a great way to ensure that you both win. Putting together the resources of both will make it a much better event and regardless of the reason that people are there, for your cause or the other one, you are still raising money for important work.

Summary
When collaborating on a marketing project, your team should work together to identify objectives, create timelines, and assign roles and responsibilities. Clear communication is essential to ensure that everyone understands their part to play and that no detail is overlooked.

Working collaboratively with others outside your organisation can also be very advantageous to your charity. Look to collaborate with organisations and individuals who are working in the same space and have similar goals. Consider local businesses, other charities, community groups, and even government agencies. This will enable the pooling of resources and manpower, ease time management pressures, and allow you to organise a bigger and better event with mutual benefits.

Timing your marketing strategy and making it easy for stakeholders to support your approach are also crucial components. Consider any key dates and events that may impact your marketing strategy, to help increase visibility and engagement with your target audience, Also be ready to take advantage of any relevant breaking news or trends on social media.

You may also be able to collaborate with micro-influencers who are genuinely interested in your cause. They can drive engagement with your organisation by amplifying your message to their followers. Provide them with a promo pack including information, graphics and videos they can use in their posts.

Action Guide: Collaboration Matrix

Overview

This worksheet is designed to help you create a collaboration matrix and establish timings for various marketing initiatives, projects, or campaigns. By completing this worksheet, you can identify key stakeholders, their roles, responsibilities, and the timeline for collaboration, ensuring smooth and efficient teamwork.

Define the Project/Campaign/Initiative

Provide a brief description of the project, campaign, or initiative that requires collaboration.

State its objectives, target audience, and proposed messaging or content.

Identify Key Stakeholders

List all individuals or teams involved in the project, campaign, or initiative (eg. marketing, sales, design, external partners).

Write their role and contact information.

Clarify Roles and Responsibilities

For each stakeholder, outline their specific roles and responsibilities within the project, campaign, or initiative.

Establish Communication Channels

Identify the preferred communication channels for collaboration (eg. email, project management tools, meetings).

Determine Project Phases or Milestones

Break down the project, campaign, or initiative into distinct phases or milestones.

Set Deadlines for Each Phase or Milestone

Assign a deadline for each phase or milestone to keep the project on track and ensure timely completion.

Assign Tasks and Deliverables

For each stakeholder, list the specific tasks and deliverables they are responsible for during each phase or milestone.

Establish Task Dependencies and Sequencing

Identify any tasks that are dependent on the completion of other tasks, and determine the appropriate sequence of activities.

Allocate Resources and Budget

Determine the resources and budget required for each stakeholder's tasks or deliverables.

Create a Timeline

Develop a visual representation of the project timeline, incorporating all phases, milestones, deadlines, tasks, and stakeholder responsibilities.

Monitor Progress and Adjust as Needed

Establish a system for tracking progress and updating the collaboration matrix and timings as needed.

Conduct Regular Check-Ins and Reviews

Schedule in advance regular check-ins or meetings with stakeholders to review progress, address any challenges, and ensure effective collaboration.

After completing this worksheet, you should have a clear collaboration matrix and timeline for your project, campaign, or initiative. Use this matrix to guide your team's efforts, monitor progress, and adjust as needed.

INTERNAL INTEGRATION

Integration is a key component of the marketing puzzle. It involves taking all the pieces, such as branding, ideation, justification, creativity, research, practical marketing ideas, collaboration, process workflows and risk management, and drawing them into a unified strategy that connects the various aspects together, thereby creating an overall marketing plan that will drive traffic and lead to the desired end goal.

Integration is about making sure that all the parts fit together in a way that is beneficial for your charity. It involves ensuring that each component is working towards the same objectives. By integrating these components, you create an effective and efficient system that allows you to increase visibility, engagement and conversions.

Integration also means looking for opportunities for automation. Automation helps streamline processes and increase efficiency. This is especially true when it comes to tasks like customer service or content creation. Automation tools can help you reduce the amount of time spent on manual processes and focus on more important tasks.

Finally, integration is important when it comes to analytics and tracking performance. A comprehensive view of your marketing efforts is important to evaluate what's working and what's not. By looking at data across all marketing plan components, you can make more informed decisions and adjust as needed.

Campaign Workflow

When it comes to marketing, having an in-depth workflow process is essential to ensure success. This is especially true when it comes to planning a strategy. Without an organised workflow, there is the risk of missing key details and components, leading to a weaker overall marketing plan. Having a thorough workflow in place helps to ensure that all aspects of the marketing plan are taken into consideration. It also helps to keep track of different tasks and responsibilities within the organisation.

When designing your workflow, there are several key steps to follow:

- *Identifying goals and objectives:* The first step is to determine what it is you are trying to accomplish with your marketing plan. It is important to consider short term and long term goals as well as how each element of the plan will contribute towards them.

- *Defining target audience:* Knowing who you want to reach is essential for successful marketing. Once you've identified your goals, you can start to define your target market and tailor your messages accordingly.
- *Assessing the channels and tools:* You need to use appropriate channels and tools to reach your target audience. This means considering which channels they are using and which tools are available to optimise your campaigns.
- *Planning content:* Content is key when it comes to marketing, so it is important to plan it out carefully. This involves creating a schedule of when and where you will be publishing content, as well as setting up regular reviews.
- *Tracking performance:* It is essential to track the performance of your campaigns so that you can assess what works and what doesn't. This will help you to tweak and optimise future campaigns for better results.

By following these steps, you can create an effective workflow process that will ensure your marketing plan runs smoothly and efficiently. With an organised workflow in place, you can ensure that all elements of your plan are taken into consideration, giving you the best chance of success.

Regular Activities

Integrating all the pieces of the marketing puzzle can be difficult but also rewarding if done correctly. By understanding the importance of each component and finding ways to ensure they are connected, you can create an effective and comprehensive marketing plan that will help drive your charity forward.

Charities are increasingly recognising the importance of marketing and communications in achieving their goals. However, all too often, these efforts are limited to a big launch event once a year, with little attention given to ongoing communication and marketing activities. This approach overlooks the value of embedding marketing and communications in everyday activities, which can lead to more sustained engagement and greater impact.

One key reason why charities should embed marketing and communications in their everyday routine is that it helps to maintain a consistent presence in the minds of stakeholders. By communicating with stakeholders regularly, a charity can build and maintain relationships that last longer than a one-off event or campaign. This can help to create a loyal base of supporters who are more likely to be invested in the charity's work and advocate for its cause.

Embedding marketing in everyday activities also allows charities to take advantage of the many opportunities that arise in the course of their work. Whether it's an upcoming event or a new initiative, there are always opportunities to communicate with stakeholders and build awareness of the charity's mission. By making communication and marketing a part of everyday activities, charities can ensure that they are always ready to take advantage of these opportunities and maximise their impact.

Charities can struggle to find the time and resources to implement effective communication and marketing strategies. However, incorporating these strategies into everyday activities provides a practical and efficient solution. By taking small steps and making conscious efforts, charities can achieve significant results and make a bigger impact. By spreading out marketing efforts over time and sending regular communications, charities can avoid the stress and burnout that often accompanies big launches. This can lead to better outcomes, as staff and volunteers are more likely to be energised and focused when they are not overwhelmed with work.

The first step in incorporating communication and marketing strategies into everyday activities is to make it a priority. Develop a clear plan and strategy, and communicate it to the team regularly. Ensure that all team members understand the importance of communication and marketing in achieving the charity's goals.

Assign specific communication and marketing roles to team members based on their strengths and interests. For example, someone who enjoys social media can be responsible for providing feedback to the charity's social media accounts, while someone who enjoys writing might like to contribute an article for the website or newsletter.

It is also critical to make use of existing resources. Charities can capitalise on their networks and partners for promotion of their activities and events. This may include sharing information about the charity on social media, mentioning the charity in newsletters or posting flyers in the premises of a partner organisation.

Incorporating communication and marketing strategies into everyday activities requires creativity and flexibility. Charities can use a variety of tactics to promote their activities and events. For instance, they can organise events that encourage community involvement, such as bake sales or charity runs. This not only raises awareness about the charity but also provides an opportunity for people to get involved and contribute.

Charities can also use email newsletters to keep supporters and donors up-to-date on the charity's activities and events. Regular newsletters can also include success stories, volunteer opportunities and other relevant information that engages and inspires supporters.

Another effective way to incorporate communication and marketing strategies into everyday activities is to utilise the power of storytelling. Charities can use stories to communicate the impact of their work and inspire supporters to take action. These stories can be shared on the charity's website, social media, newsletters and offline communication channels.

It is also vital to keep track of the impact of communication and marketing efforts. Use analytics tools to track engagement and measure the effectiveness of communication and marketing efforts. This helps to identify what works and what doesn't and enables communication and marketing strategies to be adjusted accordingly.

Moreover, charities can make use of automation tools to streamline communication and marketing processes. Automation can save time and effort while ensuring consistency in communication and branding. For example, charities can use automation tools to schedule social media posts or send newsletters.

Progress Updates

Charities often invest a significant amount of time and resources in their marketing and communication campaigns to achieve their goals. It's important to measure and report on the progress of these campaigns to stakeholders and to assess whether they are meeting their objectives. Here are some tips on how charities can report on progress and structure in their marketing campaigns:

- *Set clear and measurable objectives:* Before launching a campaign, ensure that you have clear and measurable objectives communicated internally. This will help you track progress and evaluate the success of the campaign.

- *Define and educate staff around marketing key performance indicators (KPIs):* KPIs are metrics that help you measure progress towards your objectives. They can include things like website traffic, social media engagement, email open rates and donations received.
- *Track progress regularly:* It's important to regularly track progress towards your objectives and KPIs. This will help you identify any areas that need improvement and make adjustments to the campaign if necessary.
- *Show the use of data to inform decision-making:* Data can provide valuable insights into the performance of your campaign. Analyse the data and use it to inform your decision-making process. For example, if a particular social media platform is driving the most engagement, consider focusing more resources on that platform.
- *Provide regular updates:* Keep stakeholders informed of the progress of the campaign. Provide regular updates through email newsletters, social media posts, or in-person meetings.

- *Use visuals:* Visuals can help communicate progress and data in a more engaging way. Use graphs, charts, and other visual aids to help stakeholders understand the progress of the campaign.
- *Celebrate successes:* When milestones are reached, celebrate them! This helps to motivate the team and keeps everyone focused on achieving the campaign's objectives.
- *Conduct a post-campaign evaluation:* Once the campaign is complete, conduct a thorough evaluation to assess its effectiveness. This will help you identify what worked well and what needs to be improved for future campaigns.

Exploring Automation

Automation has become a buzzword in the marketing and communication world, and for good reason. With the help of technology, organisations can streamline their marketing and communication efforts, save time and increase their efficiency. This is especially beneficial for charities, who often operate with limited resources and need to maximise their impact.

One of the most significant benefits of automation is its ability to handle repetitive and time-consuming tasks. By automating these tasks, charities can free up valuable time and resources to focus on other important aspects of their work. For example, charities can use automation to schedule social media posts, send out email newsletters, and even respond to donor inquiries. These tasks can be time-consuming and can take away from the important work of the charity. With automation, they can be handled seamlessly and efficiently.

Another benefit of automation is that it can help charities increase their reach and engagement. By using automation tools such as chatbots, charities can engage with their audience 24/7, even when their staff are not available. This can be especially useful during fundraising campaigns when donors may have questions or concerns outside of regular office hours. Additionally, automation can help charities segment their audience and deliver personalised content based on their interests and behaviour. This can help increase engagement and ultimately lead to more donations and support.

There are many tools and technologies available that charities can use to streamline their marketing and communication efforts. For example, charities can use marketing automation software to manage their email campaigns, social media, and other marketing efforts. This software allows charities to create targeted campaigns and track their success, providing valuable insights into what works and what doesn't. Additionally, charities can use customer relationship management (CRM) software to manage their donor and supporter relationships, providing a centralised system for tracking interactions and engagement.

While automation can be incredibly beneficial for charities, it is important to note that it is not a replacement for human interaction and personalisation. Charities should still strive to provide personalised and meaningful interactions with their supporters, and use automation as a tool to enhance their efforts, not replace them. Additionally, it is important to ensure that automation aligns with the charity's values and mission, and that it is used in an ethical and responsible way.

As technology continues to advance, the possibilities for automation in marketing and communication are endless. Artificial intelligence, for example, is being used by some charities to analyse data and provide insights into donor behaviour and preferences. This can help charities deliver more personalised and targeted content, leading to higher engagement and support.

Incorporating automation into a charity's marketing and communication strategy can seem daunting, but it doesn't have to be. Start by identifying the repetitive tasks that could be automated, and research the tools and technologies available. It is important to work with a reputable tool and ensure that the automation aligns with the charity's values and mission. Additionally, it is important to measure the success of the automation and make adjustments as needed.

Integration Depth

Workflows are a good measurement for marketing integration depth in a charity. Capture the steps necessary to complete a specific task or project – the right way, time after time. It's necessary to have in-depth processes to reduce human error and ensure correct workflow continuity. Clear processes minimise guesswork, reduce barriers that can slow or derail a project, and improve outcomes over time. They also reduce an organisation's reliance on individuals and their institutional memory by outlining how things get done so others can implement, too.

The checklist, a written workflow that everyone can reference, must be so simple to reference and use that it becomes standard operating procedure for the entire team. To create sustainable processes, effective branding teams develop and maintain written procedures and checklists they use consistently and repeatedly.

Workflows codify and share implicit knowledge and help ensure critical steps aren't forgotten. It is sometimes called 'processifying' – the act of mapping out, in writing, the steps necessary to successfully complete a project. Projects that involve many people and have multiple steps that impact the possible outcome benefit from 'processification'. Sorry, buzzwords*!*

Developing and using workflows requires regular moments of reflection to capture and codify essential steps so a project can be re-created efficiently and effectively in the future. Larger marketing or branding departments often have a traffic manager, project coordinator, or project manager, hired for their systems thinking and detail orientation, who is responsible for creating and adjusting the step-by-step process in writing.

Branding workflows ground a department in consistency and increase the odds that projects will turn out as planned. With that said, the most effective branding also recognises when circumstances call for something different or unusual and uses those opportunities to experiment, off-road, and learn from the experience.

Setting individual performance goals around the creation, updating, or use of workflows can motivate everyone to take them seriously. Processifying is, like many things, a muscle that is strengthened through consistent use. Celebrating wins like improved efficiency, reduced human error and downtime during staff transitions or absences, and faster project completion times can help reinforce the value of workflows over time.

Many of the tactics and projects your branding team is responsible for (sending out email newsletters, media release approach, crafting appeals, updating web pages, etc.) require following the same steps over and over again to achieve a successful outcome. When people capture these steps in writing they build institutional capacity and sustainable momentum by reducing reliance on any one person's insider expertise.

In-depth idea discovery and process building is designed to help you create a comprehensive plan for success that takes into consideration the various components of your organisation, from marketing and branding to internal marketing and beyond. With this approach, you can ensure that your organisation has the best opportunity for growth and progress in the years to come.

Depth is an approach to understanding an idea and seeing the various aspects that can be applied in order to make it successful. It involves looking into all of the different aspects of a project or idea, such as the marketing or branding, the internal marketing involved, the day-to-day integration and the overall process building.

The discovery of ideas is an essential part of any charity's marketing success. Without discovering innovative ideas and solutions to address the needs of the organisation, there will be no growth or progress. Finding great ideas is a critical part of the process, but it's not enough to just have the idea – it's also important to make sure it's fully fleshed out before you implement it. That's where depth comes in. This enables a better understanding of an idea in order to make sure that it can be implemented effectively and efficiently. It provides greater insight into how the idea can be adapted and used, and promotes better evaluation of how it can best be implemented.

Ultimately, it ensures that all aspects of the idea are taken into account, allowing for a more comprehensive understanding of the project and its potential success.

Depth is about taking the time to understand what an idea actually means from a day-to-day perspective, and how it's integrated into the regular operations of a charity. It's about thinking through all of the implications of the idea, from internal marketing to long-term goals. By taking the time to explore an idea in-depth, you can ensure that you're making an informed decision about whether or not to move forward with it. This is key to ensuring that your ideas are thoughtfully implemented and have the maximum potential to positively impact your organisation's mission. By taking the time to explore an idea in-depth, you can ensure that you are making an informed decision about whether or not to move forward with it and make sure that you are getting the most out of each and every idea.

Process building is an important tool for any organisation looking to make a lasting impression on their stakeholders and community. It ensures that all elements of an organisation's operations are running smoothly and efficiently, enabling achievement of goals more effectively.

Additionally, the activity of process building allows organisations to become more adaptable, innovative, and efficient in the long run.

By documenting processes, organisations are able to set out clear expectations and assign duties within the organisation that must be followed. This ensures that every individual knows their role and responsibilities, reducing confusion and allowing the organisation to move quickly towards its desired goals. In addition, process building can help eliminate any potential roadblocks and identify possible future issues, allowing organisations to create contingency plans and prevent problems before they arise.

Process building also allows charities to create measurable goals and assess the progress of their operations. This helps them identify areas for improvement and ensure that their efforts are aligned with their mission. The exercise of building out processes also helps streamline marketing among members of an organisation, allowing them to more easily collaborate on projects and ensure everyone has a shared understanding.

Overall, process building provides charities with the structure and transparency necessary for success. By creating clear expectations, assigning roles and responsibilities, and setting measurable goals, organisations are able to ensure that their efforts are effective and that they are able to reach their desired outcomes in a satisfactory timeframe.

Achieving depth in your charity begins with understanding the process of idea discovery and process building. It's important to evaluate the ins and outs of any potential marketing or branding idea and what it means from a day to day integration perspective.

When creating depth for your charity, start by asking yourself how this idea could further your mission and how it could help to increase engagement and donations. Take some time to research the industry, understand the target audience, and familiarise yourself with your competition. It's also important to create a plan for how you will integrate the idea into your charity organisation. Consider how this could affect internal marketing, your current operations, and whether or not it will require additional resources.

Once you have a thorough understanding of the marketing plan and the potential impact it could have on your charity organisation, it's time to test it out. Take small steps to ensure the idea works as intended before making any major changes. If the initial tests are successful, you can move forward with a larger-scale implementation.

Creating integration depth in your charity is an ongoing process. It requires patience, dedication, and a willingness to make adjustments as needed. With careful planning and strategic implementation, however, it can provide your organisation with a solid foundation for success.

Summary

Integration is a key component of the marketing puzzle. It involves taking all the pieces – branding, ideation, justification, creativity, research, practical marketing ideas, collaboration, process workflows and risk management, and drawing them into a unified strategy connecting them all together.

Having an in-depth campaign workflow process is essential to ensure success. Process building provides charities with the structure and transparency necessary for success. By creating clear expectations, assigning roles and responsibilities, and setting measurable goals, organisations can ensure their efforts are effective. In-depth process building provides greater insight into how an idea can be adapted and used, and allows for better evaluation.

Embedding marketing and communications in everyday activities can lead to more sustained engagement and allow charities to take advantage of the many opportunities that arise in the course of their work.

Opportunities to use automation in marketing and communication tasks are also expanding at a rapid rate. Integrating such technologies can help charities deliver more personalised and targeted content, leading to higher engagement and support.

Creating depth in your charity is an ongoing process. It requires patience, dedication, and a willingness to make adjustments as needed. With careful planning and strategic implementation, however, it can provide your organisation with a solid foundation for success.

Action Guide: Process and Implementation

Overview

This worksheet is designed to help you create a detailed guide and schedule for implementing your strategy. By completing this worksheet, you can establish a clear process for executing your communication initiatives, ensuring they are well-coordinated, efficient, and effective.

Define the Marketing Strategy

Provide a brief description of your communication strategy, including its objectives, target audience, key messages, tactics, and outcomes.

Break Down the Strategy into Tasks

Identify all the tasks required to execute your marketing ideas and strategy. List these tasks in a logical order or sequence.

Assign Responsibilities

Determine which individuals or teams are responsible for each task. Include their names, roles, and contact information.

Allocate Resources and Budget

Estimate the resources and budget required for each task, including personnel, materials, tools, and external services.

Set Deadlines for Each Task

Establish deadlines for the completion of each task, taking into account dependencies and sequencing.

Create a Timeline or Gantt Chart

Use these deadlines to create a schedule for your communication strategy implementation, with the start and end dates for each task, and the responsible individuals or teams.

Establish Communication Channels

Identify the preferred communication channels for collaboration and updates throughout the implementation process (eg. email, project management tools, meetings). Ensure all stakeholders are aware of and have access to these channels.

Monitor Progress and Adjust as Needed

Develop a system for tracking progress and updating the implementation schedule as necessary.

Conduct Regular Check-Ins and Reviews

Schedule regular check-ins or meetings with stakeholders to review progress, address any challenges, and ensure effective collaboration.

Evaluate the Effectiveness of the Communication Strategy

Identify key performance indicators (KPIs) that will be used to measure the success of your communication strategy.

Implement Continuous Improvement

Use the insights gained from evaluating your communication strategy to identify areas for improvement or optimisation.

Document Lessons Learned

Throughout the implementation process, document lessons learned, challenges encountered and successful practices. Use this information to improve future communication strategy implementation efforts.

After completing this worksheet, you should have a detailed guide and schedule for implementing your communication strategy. Use this guide to ensure your efforts are well-coordinated and efficient, leading to a successful execution of your communication initiatives. Remember to regularly review and adjust your plan as needed to address any challenges and maintain momentum.

RISK MITIGATION

Risk is an integral part of any marketing strategy. It involves taking calculated chances and assessing each decision's potential benefits and consequences, which may have financial, operational, reputational and legal implications for your charity.

To correctly manage risk, marketers need to understand the basic principles of risk management: risk identification, risk assessment, risk mitigation, and risk communication.

Risk identification involves analysing what types of risks might be present in your marketing plan. Risk assessment evaluates how severe each type of risk may be and assigns a risk rating accordingly. Risk mitigation entails planning how to reduce the likelihood or severity of a given risk. Finally, risk communication helps to ensure that all stakeholders are aware of the risks involved. By identifying, assessing, mitigating, and communicating risks in the context of their marketing plans, charities can better prepare for any eventualities and make sure their programs stay on track.

As marketing activities become increasingly complex, risk management processes must also evolve to keep up with changing market conditions.

There's Always Risk

Charities have the power to significantly impact society, but with great power comes great responsibility. Unfortunately, not all marketing and communication campaigns go as planned, and some can result in significant backlash from the public. It's necessary for charities to understand the potential risks involved with any activity and take steps to mitigate them to avoid damage to their reputation and mission.

One way to mitigate risk is to conduct extensive research before launching a campaign. This includes understanding the issue at hand, as well as the audience and how they are likely to receive the message. Charities should also be transparent about their motives and practices to build trust with the public. Of course, 'extensive' research sounds costly and time consuming, but allocating time to test the waters with people in, around and new to your charity can go a long way to avoiding negative public sentiment down the track.

Another way to minimise risk is to involve diverse perspectives in the planning and execution of the campaign. This includes seeking feedback and input from stakeholders, including those who may have different viewpoints or lived experiences. This can help ensure that the movement is sensitive to all perspectives and reduces the likelihood of offending or alienating any groups.

It's also important for charities to be prepared to respond quickly and effectively to any negative feedback or hostility. This includes having a crisis management plan in place and being able to address concerns or criticisms promptly and respectfully. This can help mitigate any damage to the charity's reputation and save the campaign from doing more harm than good.

Anticipating Potential Pitfalls

When planning a marketing campaign, charities must be aware that there is always a risk of backlash or antagonism. It's important to identify potential risks before launching the campaign to minimise the possibility of negative consequences.

Firstly, you need to consider your target audience. Who is your campaign aimed at? Will your message resonate with them? If your target audience feels that your campaign is insensitive, disrespectful or inauthentic, they may criticise or even boycott your charity.

Next, it's important to identify any cultural or social factors that could impact your campaign. For example, certain messages or images that may be acceptable in one country or culture could be considered offensive or inappropriate in another. Take the time to understand the cultural and social context in which your campaign will be seen.

Another factor to consider is the potential for misinterpretation. Even if your message is well-intentioned, it may be misunderstood by your audience. To minimise this risk, it's important to clearly and concisely convey your message and ensure that it cannot be misconstrued or misrepresented.

In addition, you need to consider any legal implications of your campaign. If your campaign violates any laws or regulations, it could result in legal action and damage to your charity's reputation and financial position.

Conducting a thorough risk assessment involves identifying potential risks, evaluating the likelihood of each risk occurring and assessing the potential impact of each risk. This process can help you identify and develop strategies to mitigate the most significant risks.

Seeking feedback from a diverse range of stakeholders, including members of your target audience, colleagues, and other industry professionals can help you identify any potential issues that you may have overlooked and allow you to make adjustments before launching your campaign. Sharing your plans with them and taking on board their suggestions will support the development of on-point messaging that resonates with your audience, and minimises the chance of any public backlash.

The potential for some negative consequences to occur will always exist, but don't allow this to stop your marketing activities. As long as you are open, identify possible outcomes, and take measures to better understand your audience and their expectations, you can generally ensure your communication does not do harm to your charity or community.

Marketing campaigns must always be approached with sensitivity and thoughtfulness to avoid damaging the charity's reputation and credibility. By considering factors such as the target audience, cultural and social context, legal implications, potential for misinterpretation, and conducting a thorough risk assessment, charities can minimise the risk of any negative consequences.

Worse Case Scenario

Charities, like any other organisation, can face unexpected challenges when launching a marketing campaign. Even with the best intentions and planning, things can go wrong, leading to negative publicity and public disapproval. Charities can prepare for a worst-case scenario by anticipating potential risks and developing a plan for how to respond should they occur.

The first step in preparing for the worst is to identify potential risks in your marketing campaign. Consider the possible unintended consequences of your messaging, how it could be interpreted, and the potential reactions of different stakeholder groups. Think about how you would respond if something went wrong and how you can mitigate the risks beforehand.

Once you have identified potential risks, create a crisis communication plan. This plan should include clear, simple procedures for how to respond in case of backlash or negative publicity. This plan should have a designated spokesperson who can speak on behalf of the organisation in case of crisis. It should also outline key messages that the organisation can communicate to its stakeholders, as well as a timeline for addressing the issue.

In addition to having a crisis communication plan, it's essential to develop a rapid response team (ideally a cross section of your charity) to address any potential issues as soon as they arise. This team should consist of individuals who can act quickly and effectively to address any negative feedback or concerns. The team should be prepared to provide timely and accurate information to stakeholders, and it should also have access to appropriate resources to address the issue.

Finally, always be transparent and honest in your communications with stakeholders. If something goes wrong, it's essential to admit it, take responsibility, and be transparent about what you are doing to address the issue. Honesty and transparency can go a long way in maintaining trust and credibility with your stakeholders.

While preparing for the worst-case scenario may not be the most exciting aspect of marketing and communication planning, it is essential. Involving stakeholders in the planning process, identifying potential risks, establishing a rapid response team and developing a crisis communication plan, are all important in preparing to address any issues quickly and effectively.

Transparency and honesty are critical in any communications aimed at limiting risk and responding to negative fallout. By being prepared and proactive, charities can protect their reputation and maintain the support and trust of their stakeholders and community.

Protecting Reputation

Reputation is everything in the world of charities. Without a strong reputation, it can be difficult to gain the trust of donors, volunteers and supporters, making it challenging to achieve your organisation's goals. Charities that fail to manage their reputation effectively are more likely to suffer from backlash, negative media attention and even a loss of funding. So, how can charities effectively manage their reputation?

One of the first steps is to establish a strong brand identity that is consistent across all communication channels. This includes having a clear mission statement, visual brand elements such as a logo and colour scheme, and a consistent tone and voice in all communications. By establishing a strong brand identity, charities can build trust and recognition with their audience.

Another important aspect of managing your reputation is being proactive rather than reactive. This means anticipating potential issues and addressing them before they become bigger problems. For example, if there is a risk that a particular program or initiative could be misunderstood or controversial, take steps to address these concerns in advance by providing clear and transparent information.

It's also important to be transparent in your communications with stakeholders. This means sharing both positive and negative news in a timely and honest manner. Being transparent can help to build trust and credibility, even in difficult situations.

However, despite the best efforts of charities, sometimes issues can arise that damage their reputation. In these cases, it's important to have a crisis management plan in place to effectively handle the situation. This includes having clear roles and responsibilities for managing the crisis, establishing a clear message that aligns with your brand identity, and having a plan for communicating with stakeholders.

To limit negative publicity taking a toll on donations, public trust, and the ability to achieve their goals, charities must be transparent and accountable in their actions and take swift action to address any issues or controversies that arise.

Charitable ventures often attract optimistic people who are accustomed to working toward something they believe will improve the world around them. In a positive environment, it's easy to forget that unexpected things happen sometimes. We live in a world where accidents, natural disasters, and human malice still exist. That's no doubt one of the reasons you founded or joined a charitable venture in the first place.

Make every marketing decision mindfully, and ask yourself what the results would look like a hundred years down the road. In a hundred-year charity, long-term planning is not reserved solely for the Board of Directors. Everyone involved with the charity in a decision making capacity needs to consider the long-term impact of what they do. While we all hope for the best, it is prudent to run a charity in a way that mitigates some of the most obvious risks.

Summary

Risk is an integral part of any marketing strategy. It involves taking calculated chances and assessing each decision's potential benefits and consequences, which may have financial, operational, reputational and legal implications for the organisation.

The basic principles of risk management are identification, assessment, mitigation and communication. By identifying, assessing, mitigating, and communicating risks in the context of their marketing plans, charities can better prepare for any eventualities and make sure their programs stay on track. As marketing activities become increasingly complex, risk management processes must also evolve to keep up with changing market conditions.

Risk may be mitigated by conducting extensive research before launching a campaign and by involving stakeholders with diverse perspectives in the planning and execution of the campaign. This reduces the likelihood of offending or alienating any groups.

Charities will be well placed to address any potential issues quickly and effectively if they have identified potential risks, established a rapid response team and developed a crisis communication plan. Transparency and honesty are essential in any communications aimed at limiting risk and responding to negative fallout. By being well prepared and proactive, charities can protect their reputation and maintain the support and trust of their stakeholders and community.

Action Guide: Risk Identification Chart

Overview

This worksheet is designed to help you create a risk identification chart and develop mitigation strategies for potential risks associated with your communication initiatives, projects, or campaigns. By completing this worksheet, you can proactively address potential challenges and minimise their impact on your efforts.

Define the Project/Campaign/Initiative

Provide a brief description of the project, campaign, or initiative for which you are assessing risks. State its objectives, target audience, and proposed messaging or content.

Brainstorm Potential Risks

List all potential risks that could impact the project, campaign, initiative, budget, deadlines, personnel, technology, stakeholders, and external factors.

Assign Probability and Impact

For each risk, assign a probability (likelihood) of occurrence (eg. low, medium, high), and assign a potential impact on the project, (eg. low, medium, high).

Prioritise Risks

Rank the risks based on their probability and potential impact, focusing on those with the highest combined scores. High-probability, high-impact risks should be prioritised over low-probability, low-impact risks.

Identify Risk Triggers

For each risk, determine the factors or events that could trigger its occurrence. Example: A risk trigger for budget overruns could be unexpected increases in vendor costs.

Develop Mitigation Strategies

For each prioritised risk, develop a strategy to minimise its likelihood or impact.

Example: To mitigate the risk of budget overruns, establish a contingency fund and closely monitor project expenses.

Assign Risk Owners

Designate an individual or team responsible for monitoring and managing each risk. Include their names, roles, and contact information.

Establish Monitoring and Reporting Processes

Develop a system for tracking and reporting on risks and mitigation efforts. Example: Include risk status updates in regular project meetings or status reports.

Test and Refine Mitigation Strategies

Identify ways to test your mitigation strategies to ensure their effectiveness. Refine and adjust strategies as needed based on testing results or changing conditions.

Update Risk Identification Chart and Mitigation Strategies

How will you adjust priorities and strategies as needed to maintain effective risk management?

Document Lessons Learned

Throughout the project, campaign, or initiative, document lessons learned related to risk identification and mitigation. Use this information to improve future risk management efforts.

After completing this worksheet, you should have a comprehensive risk identification chart and mitigation strategies for your project, campaign, or initiative. Use this chart to proactively address potential challenges and minimise their impact on your efforts. Regularly review and update your risk management plan to ensure its continued effectiveness and adapt to any changes in your project or environment.

IMPACT (SURPRISE!)

For charities, a habit of consistently both looking back and looking ahead helps ensure we stay on track, creating an impact beyond our own organisation and towards reaching our strategic objectives.

Taking the time and space to learn – through getting perspective, thoughtful reporting frameworks and evaluation of our marketing efforts over several months – makes us more innovative and more efficient. Such reflection is a chance to step out of the details and look around, ask ourselves if it's time to adjust course, abandon activities that no longer yield expected results, or make improvements.

Getting Perspective

Asking big picture questions will help charities stay focused and course-correct faster when required.

What do the 100 metre, 10 metre, and 1 metre views of any marketing project or initiative look like at your organisation? Is it clear where these projects or initiatives are heading? Do they align with the organisation's strategic or annual plans? Do patterns, milestones and benchmarks emerge? What must be reviewed on a weekly, monthly, quarterly, or yearly basis to ensure they stay on course?

Planning lays the foundation for practical marketing innovation as it articulates goals and desired outcomes. Marketing plans can support the organisation's primary goals, departmental objectives, and specific programs or projects. Many organisations combine something in writing (a brief, spreadsheet, dashboard or other tool) with something interpersonal (regular review meetings, debriefs, and other conversations) to reflect on the implementation of plans and tracking progress against them.

- What worked well?
- What did we do really well that we don't want to forget the next time we do this?
- What could be improved?
- What could we change?
- What didn't we do that might have worked better?
- What did we learn?

- What surprised us?
- What still puzzles us?
- What questions are not yet answered?
- How and when do we get these answers – if at all?

Questions like these remind a marketing individual, volunteer, or team to revisit its broader strategy and plans, capture and integrate lessons into its systems for future work, and course-correct if needed. They can also be useful in contexts where there is no plan.

Reporting Frameworks

Smart reporting of marketing activities helps charities uncover new strategies to achieve their organisation's goals and objectives and illuminates key variables that might otherwise have been overlooked. For charity marketing to make a positive impact a reporting framework needs to exist and be agreed upon across appropriate roles. Of course there is a balance between taking the time (and money) to research something, versus the actual resources available to do so. This will determine how detailed, segmented or varied the reporting framework will be.

For example, a large, national organisation hired a market reporting framework firm to help define its potential for membership growth. The reporting framework firm analysed existing members' profiles and identified how many other people in their community shared the same profile, clarifying the potential market for new members. Informed by specific numbers, the organisation set numeric targets to grow membership year on year that were grounded in reality, not guesswork.

Effective charities use a reporting framework to learn about the people they are trying to engage. Who are they? What inspires them to act? How do they behave? How can we reach them most effectively? Why should they care? While some organisations budget annually to conduct a market reporting framework, others do so chiefly around strategic planning or other inflection points.

It's useful to think about some of the reporting frameworks charities could conduct:

- Generative or exploratory reporting framework, which helps you identify ideas and insights, such as observations, media/ search review, or interviews.
- Descriptive and explanatory reporting framework, which helps you understand how people behave, often in qualitative ways.

- Evaluative reporting framework, which helps test what's working and what's not, such as usability testing or benchmarking.
- Causal reporting framework, which helps you come up with reasons for why something is happening, such as looking at your website's analytics to identify where visitors are coming from.
- Testing, a powerful form of evaluative reporting framework charities use, can improve results by helping you incrementally tweak the elements that inspire people to respond and engage. Will more people complete your donation landing page when there is a photograph at the top or if there are no photos? Will their average gift size change as a result? Do more people open your email newsletter when the subject line of the email features topic A or B?

An effective reporting framework begins by challenging our assumptions, and sometimes this can feel difficult when we have poured our heart and soul into a marketing approach, but if we can embrace this challenge we will enhance our marketing for the better.

How is your organisation seen and understood by the people you need to engage to advance your mission? How will they interact with you? What realities impact what they want or need from you? These assumptions are often stated (explicitly or implicitly) in the plans and project briefs communicators develop at the start of a new project, and can be an excellent basis for establishing a reporting framework.

At the start of any significant new initiative or at key junctures along the way, pressure-test your charity's assumptions (which may be rooted in implicit or explicit bias or misinformation) with a reporting framework. Use it to confirm or debunk your assumptions, define the intangible, and illuminate the best path forward.

The Next Three Months

Marketing innovation is a powerful component of a charity's work; it reports trends, publishes research and media topics, and invites collaboration with other individuals and groups responding to similar problems. Deeper marketing analysis, insights, and integration can create enhanced experiences and help the entire charity – not just its marketing team – improve.

Marketing science, the discipline of analysing marketing results to answer questions and reveal insights, is a relatively new field that is increasingly making its way into the charity sector.

Not all organisations need marketing scientists or people with advanced technical skills who can build complex algorithms. Marketing staff and their peers in programs, development, and other departments can collaborate to ask key questions, make sure that the Idea they capture and use is stored and maintained effectively, and create moments of marketing innovation that yield insights.

- Compare your marketing results to peers: Are your outcomes comparable to, greater than, or less than those of other organisations? Are you smashing it or lagging behind in your sphere?
- *Measure results:* Did you achieve what you set out to do? Is the work lining up to your strategic objectives? Enlisting other charities to assist with marketing analysis can help your organisation gather insights gained from the work of one specific department and apply them organisation-wide. Effective charities can translate these lessons into audience profiles and mindsets, craft brand assets that are more compelling, and share lessons learned with everyone in that organisation.

Aggregating marketing into scorecards and dashboards: Each department or section of a charity has its own key performance indicators (KPIs) and metrics depending on the make up of a charity. Fundraisers might track retention rates, lifetime value, while others track donor behaviour, commitment, and engagement. Program teams track how many people apply, accept, attend, and return. Marketing is uniquely positioned to share insights across the organisation and to report on overall engagement with the mission. Creating a scorecard or dashboard that includes organisation-wide objectives will provide a solid step into the future – being mindful of how other goals are tracking and interplaying as a result (or not) of your marketing efforts.

Marketing may also track external awareness of the organisation and its mission more generally, measuring how well-known and understood the brand is. Dashboards and scorecards provide perspective for moments of constructive marketing innovation by revealing patterns and shifts in KPIs over time. By reviewing measurable activities about how people are engaging on a weekly or monthly basis, your team can identify what's working well and where improvements could be made, and spot trends when things change.

Measuring Impact

As a charity, you are passionate about making a difference in the world. But how do you measure the impact of your work? Impact is the difference your organisation makes in the lives of the people you serve and the communities in which you work. It's the positive change you create and the progress you achieve towards your mission.

When it comes to your marketing and communication strategy, impact is essential. It's what inspires donors, volunteers, and stakeholders to support your cause. By showing the impact of your work, you can demonstrate the value of your organisation and build trust with your audience.

So, how can you ensure your marketing and communication strategy reflects your impact? It starts with defining your goals and the outcomes you hope to achieve. Consider what success looks like for your organisation and the people you serve. What change do you want to create in the world?

Next, think about how you can measure your impact. This may include collecting data, conducting surveys, or tracking key performance indicators. By measuring your impact, you can understand the effectiveness of your work and identify areas for improvement.

Once you have a clear understanding of your impact, it's time to incorporate it into your marketing and communication strategy. Use data and statistics to illustrate the impact of your work and the positive results you've achieved. But impact isn't just about the numbers. It's also about the emotional connection you create with your audience. Use storytelling to bring your impact to life and engage your audience on a deeper level. Highlight the personal stories of people you've helped, the progress you've made towards your mission, and the real-world change you're creating.

It's important to remember that impact is not a once only achievement. It's an ongoing process that requires constant evaluation and improvement. Continuously assess your impact and adjust your strategy to ensure you're realising the outcomes you set out to achieve.

By prioritising impact in your marketing strategy, you can build a powerful brand and inspire action towards your mission. Remember, impact is not just about what you do, but the difference you make in the world. So, take the time to reflect on your impact and use it as a driving force in all aspects of your organisation.

Evaluating the effectiveness of a marketing idea or strategy is crucial for charities to ensure that they are achieving their goals and making a meaningful impact. But how do you go about this?

- *Set clear goals:* Before launching a campaign, charities should set clear goals that are specific, measurable, achievable, relevant, and time-bound. This will help them track their progress and determine if their marketing strategy is effective in achieving those goals.
- *Monitor key performance indicators (KPIs):* Charities should monitor key performance indicators such as website traffic, social media engagement, email open and click-through rates, and fundraising conversion rates. These metrics will help them understand how their audience is engaging with their content.
- *Collect feedback:* Charities should actively seek feedback from their stakeholders, including donors, volunteers, and beneficiaries. This feedback can be collected through surveys, focus groups or personal conversations. Feedback can help charities

understand how their strategy is resonating with their audience and identify areas for improvement.

- *Analyse data:* Charities should analyse data collected from various sources, such as social media analytics tools, website analytics, and email marketing software. This analysis will help them understand how their strategy is performing and identify trends and patterns in audience behaviour.
- *Conduct A/B testing:* A/B testing involves testing different versions of a marketing message or campaign with a sample audience to determine which version is more effective. This type of testing can help charities optimise their strategy for better results.
- *Use case studies:* Charities can use case studies to evaluate the effectiveness of their strategy. Case studies involve interviewing beneficiaries or donors to understand how the charity's marketing content has impacted them. These case studies can be used to illustrate the impact of the charity's work and help refine the strategy.
- *Evaluate the return on investment (ROI):* Charities should evaluate the ROI of their strategy, ie. the financial return of the investment in relation to the cost of that investment. This will help determine if their

marketing strategy is delivering a positive financial return and identify areas where this may be improved.

Finally, it's essential to regularly review and update your marketing strategy to ensure it stays relevant and effective. As your organisation grows and your audience evolves, your strategy should evolve as well. Be open to trying new tactics and channels, and be willing to adjust your strategy as needed to continue making an impact. This way, you can ensure you're making the biggest impact possible and effectively communicating your message to your audience.

Assess progress regularly to ensure your marketing engine continues to run smoothly. Periodically seek input from staff about whether your marketing is achieving the desired outcomes. Repeat the self-assessment every year and update your marketing strategy and plan as needed.

Every new tool, enhanced process, or sharper strategy that you put in place will help your nonprofit's marketing engine grow stronger, as will every person who augments your team and positively shapes the culture. Incremental progress is the only, and perhaps best, way to do this work. Over time, the results will be clear and profound. Progress – not perfection – is the key.

Flexibility and Workflow

In today's rapidly changing world, it is crucial for charities to be flexible and willing to pivot their marketing and communications strategy if necessary. But how can a charity know when it's time to pivot, and how should they communicate this change to their team?

The first step is to regularly monitor and evaluate the effectiveness of your current strategy. Are you meeting your goals and reaching your target audience? Are there any metrics or feedback that suggest a change is needed? Keeping track of this information will help you recognise when it's time to pivot.

Once you've identified the need to pivot, it's important to communicate this change to your team as soon as possible. Transparency is key, and the earlier you communicate the need to pivot, the more time your team will have to adjust to the new strategy.

When communicating the change, it's important to be clear about the reasons behind the pivot and the new direction you will be taking. This will help your team understand the rationale and get on board with the new approach.

An effective way to communicate this change internally is through a team meeting or presentation. Use this opportunity to explain the changes, answer questions, and give your team the chance to provide feedback and ask for clarification. By involving your team in the pivot process, they will feel more invested in the new strategy and more likely to support its success.

It's also important to modify your external messaging to reflect the new strategy. This may include updating your website, social media accounts, and other marketing materials to ensure they align with the new direction. You may also need to reach out to your target audience to explain the change and how it will benefit their work and mission.

When modifying your marketing and communications strategy, it's important to remain true to your charity's core values and mission. This will ensure that your audience understands the authenticity of your message and remains loyal to your cause.

Many charities become dependent on individuals who manage and execute marketing projects, putting sustainable momentum in jeopardy. Exploring these questions can help you determine if you've built a marketing engine that can function independently of key people:

- Do we have documented marketing workflows and systems that help our team execute projects effectively? Can new people quickly get up to speed on the work?
- Are the workflows regularly updated, referenced, and maintained?
- Are we dependent on a few people with 'corporate' memory or specialised knowledge to get things done? How can this be captured and stored?
- Would we be able to communicate well if key people left the charity unexpectedly – without rebuilding from scratch?

If the answers to these questions reveal a lack of sustainable momentum, start by defining processes that will enable your team to work more efficiently and build capacity. People who lead marketing projects or teams might not have any formal project management background. With a little professional development they'll see the value of creating tools, workflows, and systems that can be used without relying on any single individual.

Summary

The practice of consistently both looking back and looking ahead helps ensure charities stay on track. Taking the time and space to learn – through getting perspective, thoughtful reporting frameworks and evaluation of our marketing efforts – makes us more innovative and more efficient.

A reporting framework is essential. Smart reporting of marketing activities illuminates key variables that might otherwise have been overlooked and helps charities uncover new strategies to achieve their goals.

Building engagement, communicating with a clear voice, and creating sustainable momentum are not one-off achievements. Maintaining a marketing engine in good working order requires ongoing focus. Every new tool, enhanced process, or sharper strategy that you put in place will help your charity's marketing grow stronger.

Impact is the difference your organisation makes in the lives of the people you serve. It's the positive change you create. By prioritising impact in your marketing strategy, you can build a powerful brand and inspire action towards your mission.

It's essential to regularly review and update your marketing strategy to ensure it stays relevant and effective. As your organisation grows and your audience evolves, your strategy should evolve as well. Be open to trying new tactics and channels to continue making an impact.

What's Next?

Marketing is an essential part of any charity's success, and the strategies used to achieve that success must be dynamic and ever-changing. There is an expiration date on marketing ideas and strategies because the world around us is constantly evolving, and what may have worked a few months ago may no longer be effective. This is why it is essential to conduct a review of your marketing and comms strategies every 6-12 months to ensure that they are still effective and relevant.

The first step in conducting a review is to assess the performance of your current strategy. This can be done by looking at key performance indicators (KPIs) such as website traffic, social media engagement, email open rates, and conversion rates. These KPIs can help you determine the effectiveness of your strategy and identify areas for improvement.

After identifying areas for improvement, it is time to pivot and modify your strategy. This can involve anything from adjusting your messaging to incorporating new tactics or channels. It is important to remember that the goal of modifying your strategy is not to completely overhaul it but rather to make targeted adjustments that will improve its effectiveness.

Communicate any changes in strategy internally as soon as possible, through a team meeting or all-hands call. Provide a clear explanation of why the changes are being made and what the expected outcomes are, and allow team members the opportunity to ask questions and provide feedback. It is also a good idea to follow up with an email or memo summarising the changes and outlining the next steps. This will help ensure that everyone on your team is on the same page and working towards the same goals.

When conducting a review and making changes to your strategy, ensure that you are staying up-to-date with the latest trends and best practices in marketing and communication. Where possible attend industry conferences and make some time each week to read industry publications and network with charities in your field.

Finally, approach the review and renewal of your strategy with a growth mindset. Recognise that there is always room for improvement and that your strategy must evolve over time to remain effective. With a willingness to experiment, take risks, and adapt to change, your charity can start (or continue) to effectively communicate its message and achieve its goals – and play its part in making the world a better place.

Action Guide: Impact Potential

Overview

This worksheet is designed to help you create an impact potential map for your marketing initiatives, projects, or campaigns. By completing this worksheet, you can identify the best and worst-case scenarios; key points in between; reporting requirements; and alignment with organisational strategy; allowing you to better anticipate outcomes and adjust your approach accordingly.

Define the Project/Campaign Initiative

Provide a brief description of the project, campaign, or initiative for which you are assessing impact potential. State its objectives, target audience, and proposed messaging or content.

Identify Organisational Strategy Alignment

Describe how the project, campaign, or initiative aligns with your organisation's overall strategy or goals. Explain the expected benefits or value it will bring to the organisation.

Determine Worst Case Scenario

Identify the worst possible outcome(s) for your project, campaign, or initiative.

Example: The campaign fails to generate any leads, resulting in wasted resources and a negative impact on the company's reputation.

Identify Factors Contributing to the Worst Case Scenario

List the factors or events that could contribute to the worst-case scenario occurring.

Example: Insufficient budget, poorly targeted messaging, ineffective promotional channels.

Develop Contingency Plans for Worst Case Scenario

Create plans to address the factors contributing to the worst-case scenario, minimising its likelihood or impact.

Example: Allocate additional budget, conduct thorough audience research, test multiple promotional channels.

Determine Best Case Scenario

Identify the best possible outcome(s) for your project, campaign, or initiative.

Example: The campaign generates a significant number of high-quality leads, resulting in increased sales and a positive ROI.

Identify Factors Contributing to the Best Case Scenario

List the factors or events that could contribute to the best-case scenario occurring.

Example: Adequate budget, well-targeted messaging, effective promotional channels.

Develop Action Plans for Best Case Scenario

Create plans to capitalise on the factors contributing to the best-case scenario, maximising its likelihood or impact.

Example: Ensure sufficient budget allocation, invest in audience research, and optimise promotional channels.

Map Key Points in Between

Identify the key points or milestones between the worst and best-case scenarios. Describe the factors, events, or decisions that could lead to these intermediate outcomes.

Establish Reporting Requirements

Determine the key performance indicators (KPIs) or metrics that should be reported on to track progress and outcomes.
Example: Leads generated, conversion rate, ROI.

Monitor Progress and Adjust as Needed

Regularly review progress and outcomes, comparing them to the impact potential map.

After completing this worksheet, you should have a comprehensive impact potential map for your project, campaign, or initiative. Use this map to anticipate outcomes, adjust your approach, and ensure alignment with organisational strategy. Regularly review and update your impact potential map to maintain its relevance and adapt to changing circumstances.

BONUS: CHARITY MARKETING TOOLBOX

Why 26 Marketing Ideas?

The dynamic landscape of modern marketing offers a vast array of opportunities to charities, both big and small. While many may argue that the corporate world has been swift to harness the potential of new-age strategies, the charity sector is in no way lagging behind. The inherent goal of charities provides them with a unique positioning that can be leveraged through effective marketing. But with so many strategies available, where should we begin?

Let's set the record straight: the list of marketing ideas presented here is not a stringent roadmap that every charity should follow to the letter. Rather, it's like a marketplace brimming with stalls of different colours, sizes, and offers. Each stall represents a unique marketing idea, waiting to be explored and perhaps, adopted.

Just as you might walk through a market, pausing to look at items, maybe trying a few, and then choosing what suits you best, the same philosophy applies to these marketing strategies. There's no 'one-size-fits-all'. Each charity has its ethos, its target audience, its constraints and its strengths. The art is in identifying which of these strategies aligns best with your organisational values, strategic goals, budget, people power and of course – the cause you're driving to impact.

The beauty of the diverse list is that it acts as a starting point. It's a gentle nudge, prompting you to think, evaluate, and perhaps, innovate. Whether you're a novice to the world of marketing or a seasoned campaigner, there's always something new to learn and adapt. The digital age, with its ever-evolving platforms and trends, ensures that the learning never stops.

So why 26 ideas? When I first started working with charities, I would give myself a fortnight to learn something new in the marketing world, come up with a way to trial it and even implement it in that time. Whether you go this far or not, using 15-20 minutes each fortnight to at least read about one of the marketing ideas here gives you a year's worth of marketing potential, and hopefully – impact potential.

Ask yourself: Is there a strategy here that resonates with our mission? Have we tried a variant of one of these ideas? If yes, how did it fare? Could we tweak it for better results? Or perhaps, is there a strategy that we haven't considered before, but feels right to explore now?

In addition, this list aims to encourage a culture of regular evaluation. In the hustle and bustle of campaign launches, fundraising drives, grant application, and community outreach, it's easy to fall into the trap of routine. However, the most successful charities are those that continually assess their strategies, learning from both their successes and failures. If you're already implementing one or more of the ideas from the list, use it as an opportunity to pause and reflect. Are there improvements to be made? New angles to consider?

The emphasis here is not on the number of strategies adopted, but rather on their quality, relevance, and impact. A charity might find that diving deep into just three or four of these ideas over the course of a year yields more meaningful results than skimming the surface of ten.

Treat this compilation of marketing strategies as a compass – there to suggest directions, guide and inspire. So, as you step forward, embracing the world of possibilities that charity marketing presents, remember that it's all about finding what resonates with your strategy. Here's to impactful storytelling, meaningful connections, and a brighter, better world shaped by the relentless efforts of charities and the people within them.

To further assist you in navigating these strategies, each idea is accompanied by a short overview. This includes a clear starting point or the next step you can immediately take. There's a glimpse into what a basic, traditional approach might entail. For the adventurous, there is also a more ambitious, 'push the limits' method that dares you to think outside the box and make a bigger splash. And as every strategy unfolds, it's vital to gauge its effectiveness. Hence, each one has delineated success criteria, helping you determine if you're on the right track, or if you need to pivot. This structured approach ensures that you have a holistic view, whether you're taking your first step or elevating your game.

1. First Step
2. Traditional approach
3. Push the limits
4. Success indicator

The suggestions following are ordered so as to begin with generally familiar strategies, moving progressively towards ideas that may be new or less familiar to you.

1. Community Radio, Tv and School Newsletters

Charities may promote their causes and raise awareness via airtime on community radio and television, and through school newsletters. Because of the local nature of these platforms, organisations may reach large demographics with a high level of interest in the causes they support or the services they provide. Charities may spread their ideas far and wide via such channels without breaking the bank on advertising.

This approach entails several benefits. These channels put organisations in touch with local audiences involved in their own neighbourhoods and hence more willing to donate to community-based causes. Local voices are more likely to build trust and support for a charity organisation.

Advertising on community television and radio needs solid preparation. To make the most of these platforms:

- Find community radio and television stations in your region as a starting point for your research. Try to determine whether their programming style, audience, special interests and focus areas are a suitable match for your organisation.

• Connect with the station's management and personnel to get insight into their programming needs and preferences. Getting to know the right people and earning their trust may pave the door for future partnerships and reveal the most effective ways of engaging their audience.

• Create an interesting selling point: Develop a distinct, interesting concept for a show or segment that fits in with the station's programming and would interest the station's audience. Make sure the material you suggest is something that people want to hear or see and that they will learn something from.

• Ensure you are organised and well prepared. Gather whatever media you'll need to illustrate your point, whether that's audio or visual, and be ready to deliver it. Your pitch will have greater weight with station officials if you present yourself in a professional manner.

• After presenting your concept to the station's management, keep in contact with them to offer updates and answer any questions they may have. Keeping the lines of communication open will help to establish your company's continued patronage.

It's important to think about the potential drawbacks as well. For charities looking to maximise their impact, a narrow broadcasting presence that keeps their message confined to a limited, localised audience may not be optimal. Furthermore, small organisations may struggle to generate and deliver interesting material for radio or television due to limited funding and manpower.

It can be difficult to secure airtime on local radio and television stations. It takes perseverance, patience and flexibility to propose ideas, cultivate connections and create content.

Advertising via school newsletters is another avenue to access a captive audience consisting of parents, students, and school employees. These newsletters are sent on a regular basis and make it possible to inform many people of your charity's current activities.

As with community radio and TV, finding the correct people to send your message to is the first step. Contributing to school newsletters requires contacting the appropriate administrators, be they teachers, principals or parent organisations.

Highlight the importance of your charity's goals and achievements. Be sure that your message is clear and to the point. Visuals like photos and videos will help your audience connect with and remember your content. Make it easy for readers to take action in support of your cause by providing a link to your website.

Action 1: Community Radio and TV

First Step: Research local community radio or TV stations and their contact details.

Traditional: Propose a monthly segment discussing your charity's impact, targeting a consistent 5,000 listeners/viewers.

Push the Limits: Organise a charity takeover day on the station with interviews, stories, and music, aiming for 20,000 listeners/viewers.

Success Indicator: Audience metrics, feedback from segments and success of the takeover day.

Action 2: School Newsletters

First Step: Identify 5 local schools and get in touch with their administration or parent council.

Traditional: Share an article or update on your charity for the next school newsletter, targeting 3 publications in the next two months.

Push the Limits: Organise an educational event or workshop in partnership with a school and promote it via the newsletter, aiming for 500 attendees.

Success Indicator: Inclusions in school newsletters, feedback from parents and event attendance.

2. Facebook and Real Time Social Media

A Facebook group is a great way to connect with other supporters of your charity and grow your organisation's online presence. You can build loyalty and increase contributions from members by communicating with them, answering their issues and concerns, and demonstrating your gratitude for their support.

This may be a great way to spread the word about your charity. Building a group of people who have an interest in your cause allows you to connect with them on a deeper level, which in turn increases the likelihood that they will stick with your organisation over the long term.

Creating a Facebook group begins with settling on a mission and target demographic. Take care to choose a name that appeals to your intended followers and conveys your organisation's mission effectively. New members may benefit from a welcome letter outlining the group's goals and ground rules.

Post updates on the organisation's development, offer motivational stories and quotations, and invite members to submit their own insights. Volunteers may be sought, fundraising efforts promoted, and forthcoming events announced via this group.

Keep in mind, however, that running a Facebook group isn't a walk in the park. To maintain the group's interest and activity, you'll need to be regular in your contributions and responses. You'll also need to keep a close eye on things to make sure everyone in the group is always treated with dignity and respect.

Connecting with supporters and finding new donations may be facilitated tremendously by using live and real-time social media. Live video streaming and real-time chats allow charities to provide their supporters unprecedented insight into their efforts and activities. A charity might broadcast live to announce a new initiative, talk about an inspiring success story or explain how their organisation works in action. Inspiring prospective contributors to take action by appealing to their emotions is much easier with this kind of information.

To get things rolling, charities need to make sure they're actively interacting with their social media followers on a consistent basis. Demonstrating that you respect their input will help gain the confidence and loyalty of your followers.

Online visibility and marketing effectiveness can be enhanced by using paid promotions for postings and live video streaming, focusing on certain groups or topics of interest.

Action: Facebook/Real Time Social Media
First Step: Choose an upcoming event or day-to-day activity to live-stream.
Traditional: Host a monthly live Q&A session, aiming to engage 200 viewers consistently.
Push the Limits: Organise a 'Day in the Life' live stream, capturing various aspects of the charity, targeting 1000 views.
Success Indicator: Number of live viewers, engagement during streams and feedback from the audience.

3. A Promotional Kit

Charities can capitalise heavily on promotional toolkits, also known as media kits or press kits, to spread their mission to a larger audience.
One of the best reasons to put up a promotional toolkit is to ensure your company's message is consistent across all channels. When all members of an organisation have the same understanding of its goals, it's much simpler to advocate for those

goals and principles. By maintaining a constant tone and voice, a charity may gain the confidence of its target audience and attract additional financial backing, volunteers and strategic alliances.

Key statements that identify and express the charity's mission should be included in the promotional kit. An overview of the group, its goals, the justifications for its actions, and opportunities for participation should all be included. It's also important to provide a way for people to get in touch with the organisation and find out more information, so be sure to include links to your website and social media pages.

Include printed items, such as brochures, posters and other collateral in your kit, as many people still like to have printed information to refer to. This can provide additional details about initiatives and activities. With such information at their fingertips, vendors, partners, and other supporters may better understand the charity's mission and easily share information.

When drawing up a promotional kit, it's important to think about the possible downsides as well as the benefits. The expense of creating and delivering high-quality printed materials is a major obstacle. Organisations with smaller budgets may have difficulty allocating resources for this purpose, bearing in mind that it may limit their overall promotional efforts.

Another challenge is making sure promotional materials always reflect the most recent facts. They need to be regularly revised and updated to reflect the organisation's current programmes and efforts, which can be time consuming. For smaller organisations with fewer resources, this kind of routine upkeep may entail a significant administrative strain.

Finally, although a promotional kit may do a good job of communicating a charity's mission and values, it should not be used in isolation. To have the greatest possible effect, organisations should use a multifaceted marketing plan that makes use of a wide range of tools, such as online and offline media, live events and public relations campaigns.

Action Details: Promotional Kit

First Step: Design a basic promotional kit template (eg. using a free online graphic design tool), including key charity information, within the next two weeks.

Traditional: The kit should include brochures, impact reports, and a personalised letter, aiming to reach 50 stakeholders in the next month.
Push the Limits: Include interactive elements like a digital component (QR codes leading to a video or virtual tour) or unique charity merchandise, aiming to enhance stakeholder engagement by 30%.
Success Indicator: Number of kits distributed, feedback from stakeholders, and increase in stakeholder engagement or donations.

4. Recruit Volunteers

Recruiting volunteers to help with marketing is a great method for charities to boost their marketing efforts and brand recognition. Volunteer marketing assistants may fill the void that exists due to the inability of certain charities to recruit full-time, qualified marketers. *GoodCompany* (an Australian platform that empowers professionals to donate their time, talents and money to charity) facilitates communication between charitable organisations and people all around the globe who are willing to give their time and share their expertise online.

There are numerous ways in which volunteer marketing assistants might aid charities. Depending on their personal skills, they can provide support in a wide variety of areas, including content production, visual design, social media management, website building, search engine optimisation (SEO) and data analytics. Putting their knowledge to good use may lead to increased brand awareness, consumer participation and financial contributions.

Signing up for *GoodCompany* and creating a project profile explaining your organisation's aims is all that's required to get started. After the profile has been published, the organisation may start accepting suggestions from prospective volunteer marketers. Once a qualified volunteer marketing assistant is located, the platform requires no payment or further commitment.

Action: Recruit Volunteers
First Step: Create a list of roles where volunteers could significantly impact your charity.
Traditional: Post on local community boards and websites, aiming to onboard 20 volunteers in the next month.
Push the Limits: Host a 'volunteer marathon' day with workshops, aiming to attract 100 volunteers.
Success Indicator: Number of new volunteers onboarded, their engagement level, and feedback from the marathon event.

5. Email Newsletters

Charities may reach and educate their audience with the use of email newsletters, a powerful marketing tool. These provide a simple and inexpensive channel of contact for interacting with current and new donors alike. A well-written and strategically distributed email newsletter can do wonders for your charity's visibility, readership, and eventual success.

It's crucial to think about your intended readers and their interests when you construct your email newsletter. Your website's content may include news about current and forthcoming events and initiatives, personal accounts from volunteers and employees, expressions of gratitude from those who have benefited from your work and informative resources linked to your cause. Keeping your readers interested and building their loyalty to your cause may be accomplished via a combination of educational and motivational posts.

Choosing to publish the newsletter once every three months helps you to save time and energy by focusing on the most important information for that time period. A library of previously collected articles and news items may provide a plethora of material for use in subsequent newsletters. To further ensure that your email is relevant and useful to your audience, it is important to routinely get feedback from readers.

The free price tag is a key reason for their popularity. Email newsletters are a cost-effective alternative to more conventional print marketing tools for organisations. In addition, you can quickly and easily reach a huge audience, while receiving immediate responses on engagement metrics like open rates, click-through rates and conversions.

Email newsletters also allow you to divide your readership into subsets based on demographics, past engagement and more. Providing members with information that is more tailored to their interests will increase engagement and cement your connection with them.

However, given the average person's daily email volume, it might be difficult to make your message stand out. You may overcome this if your newsletter genuinely helps your readers and uses catchy subject lines to attract their attention.

A healthy mailing list is crucial to the success of email newsletters. Constantly updating and expanding your list might be taxing on your time and energy, but if you want to avoid legal trouble and operate in accordance with privacy standards, you need to be sure that your newsletter subscribers have actively chosen to receive it.

Action: Email Newsletters
First Step: Survey your current subscribers to find out what they'd like more of in your newsletter.
Traditional: Introduce a monthly spotlight on success stories, aiming for a 20% increase in open rates.
Push the Limits: Organise a monthly giveaway or exclusive content for subscribers, targeting a 15% growth in subscribers within two months.
Success Indicator: Open rates, subscriber growth, and feedback on new content.

6. *Social Proof*

Incorporating social proof and testimonials into your marketing strategy is an effective way of demonstrating the influence and legitimacy of your charity organisation, over time establishing trust and strengthening ties with prospective donors. Credibility is established by the use of case studies and anecdotes from volunteers, contributors or beneficiaries, all of whom can attest to the validity of your organisation's work and the success which it continues to build upon. Trust is promoted through showing that others have had similar experiences and have gained confidence in your organisation's services. The stories you share will foster a personal connection with people, resulting in further involvement and increased donations.

Testimonials and social proof are versatile marketing tools since they may be used in a wide range of contexts, from websites and social media to email newsletters and fundraising initiatives.

However, reaching out to contributors, volunteers and recipients; and collecting images and making videos, may take a lot of time and energy. Be aware that some people remain wary of testimonials, so avoid using them too much. And when publishing reviews, avoid highlighting only positive feedback, or you may damage your company's credibility.

Remember that it is vital to obtain peoples' permission before publishing stories about their experiences and crucial to protect their privacy.

Action: Social Proof
First Step: Collate 5 testimonials or success stories from beneficiaries or supporters.
Traditional: Share these on your primary communication channels, targeting a 10% increase in engagements.
Push the Limits: Create a multimedia campaign around real-life success stories, aiming for a 30% uplift in audience reach.
Success Indicator: Engagement on social proof content, growth in audience reach, and feedback on multimedia campaigns.

7. Membership Benefits

Offering contributors exclusive access via a membership programme is an excellent way to increase your organisation's patronage. Memberships may bring in consistent funds for your organisation since donors are enticed to make recurring payments in return for benefits. Membership benefits may increase support for your charity by creating a feeling of appreciation, exclusivity, loyalty and involvement, encouraging continued support.

You can give your organisation more recognition and exposure by distributing branded goods to your members, such as apparel or other items with logos. Make sure the rewards you offer are appealing and timely, as there are sure to be other groups vying for members' time and money, particularly if other charities provide comparable benefits.

The drawbacks of promoting your organisation through memberships include a substantial administrative overhead which may necessitate additional manpower and resources.

While memberships can foster an exclusive atmosphere, they should not come at the expense of non-members or make them feel second-rate.

Remember, not everyone who makes a donation wants something in return and may actually be offended by the suggestion.

Action: Membership Benefits

First Step: Identify 3 benefits or rewards that members/donors would value.

Traditional: Offer a monthly e-newsletter with exclusive updates and opportunities, aiming to retain 90% of the current member base.

Push the Limits: Organise an exclusive annual members-only event with notable guests, targeting 70% member attendance.

Success Indicator: Membership retention rate, feedback on the benefits and event attendance.

8. Other Local Charities, Community Groups and Businesses

If your charity is on a very limited budget, partnering with other organisations in the area may be a very effective method of promotion. By forming strategic alliances with other charities, community groups or even local businesses that have complementary missions, convictions or customer bases, you may double the impact of your marketing campaigns. Projects, events, and networking opportunities are just some of the ways in which organisations may work together and support one another.

Working together has several benefits for both groups, including reducing expenses, reaching more people, and raising public awareness about pressing problems. Collaboration with other organisations with a similar mission may also help build a stronger charity sector by encouraging a feeling of community and the exchange of ideas and resources.

Seek to collaborate with those charities or organisations whose missions best align with your own. By working together in this way, you can pool your abilities and resources to make a more significant impact in your locality. There may be ways to work together productively even where your organisations have differing objectives.

Where two organisations host or participate in a fundraiser, event, or social media campaign together, more people will hear about their work and support for both is likely to increase. Together, you may deliver more value to your target audience via joint projects, such as creating a website or app that highlights the strengths and capabilities of both organisations. It is essential that any partnership provides results for both parties and mutual promotion should be undertaken in a friendly manner. Cooperation in marketing is more efficient and fruitful than competition for the same customers and resources.

However, it's important to think about the possible downsides as well. Your charity's capabilities may be stretched thin by the time and energy required to manage a relationship, particularly if you have a small team and a restricted budget. Before committing to a partnership, it's crucial to weigh the possible return on investment and the compatibility of aims and ideals.

In addition, your charity's brand and message may be watered down by joining up with another charity, since donors may have trouble telling the two apart. Furthermore, conflict or misunderstanding might arise from differences in organisational culture, beliefs, or techniques, which can ultimately hinder the effectiveness of joint marketing activities.

Action: Other Local Organisations
First Step: Connect with two local charities, community groups or businesses through *LinkedIn* or direct email.
Traditional: Jointly host community drives or campaigns, targeting a 25% increase in combined volunteer participation.

Push the Limits: Create a shared online platform or event to amplify both missions, aiming to engage 10,000 individuals in the next two months.
Success Indicator: Joint events hosted, participation rates, and combined platform engagement.

9. Youtube Videos

The development of free and powerful social media channels has completely altered the way charities interact with their supporters. *YouTube* is one such site that may be used to great advantage by charitable organisations to spread information about their work, increase awareness and gain funding. Making an engaging video for *YouTube* doesn't need a big budget or famous actors; all you need is a solid script, some patience and a message that comes across loud and clear.

First, think about the mission of your charity and the message you want to send. This might be an overview of your organisation's goals, a description of the services you provide and how they help people, or a poignant account of how your charity has impacted the lives of its recipients. Make sure your intended audience can relate to and be interested in your message.

The next step is to write a script that captures attention and gets the point across. Don't forget to include a strong call to action at the conclusion, encouraging viewers to help your cause by sharing, giving, or volunteering. Once you have finished writing your script, recruit people who are enthusiastic about helping you realise your vision. Volunteers from the organisation or the community at large might serve as actors or narrators to reduce production expenses.

Several freely available programs and websites, such as *Animoto*, can help in the video production process. Make sure your video is both aesthetically appealing and emotionally stirring by carefully picking the music, visuals, and effects that will serve to deliver your message.

YouTube can be a powerful tool in your charity's social media arsenal, generating connections and rallying support for your cause. Videos also have a larger potential audience since they are simple to share online in a variety of formats.

However, using *YouTube* for promotional purposes in the charity sector is not without its downsides. Charities with few resources may find it difficult to dedicate the time and energy required to create and manage a successful *YouTube* channel. The sheer volume of posts also makes it difficult for charities to get people's attention. The impact of these challenges may be mitigated by paying to promote content on other social media platforms, and by using keyword analysis and tagging to improve the visibility of the charity's videos in search engines.

Action: YouTube Videos

First Step: Identify a key message or story you want to share about your charity.

Traditional: Start by creating a series of informational videos detailing your charity's work, with a goal of reaching 1,000 views in the first month.

Push the Limits: Organise a live telethon-style fundraiser on *YouTube*, with guest appearances, aiming for 10,000 live viewers.

Success Indicator: View count, subscriber growth, and funds raised during the telethon.

10. Thank You Letters

Charities may show their appreciation to their donors in a meaningful manner by sending them a handwritten letter. This kind of individual attention may go a long way towards cementing loyal support from your organisation's benefactors. It is essential to be heartfelt, specific, and prompt when writing a letter of gratitude. In the thank-you note, be sure to outline the donor's gift and emphasise the positive change it will bring about.

Physical thank-you notes are a great method to show your appreciation to contributors and keep them updated of the organisation's progress. You may use this time to inform people on your progress, tell them inspiring stories of the individuals you've helped and demonstrate the impact of their donations. This will foster stronger investment in your cause and increase loyalty to your organisation.

A handwritten thank-you note will also help your charity stand out from others that only use automated email thank-you systems. Supporters will know you appreciate them and their donations more because you have taken the time to write them a thoughtful, individual message, and will encourage future contributions. Keeping your supporters informed about forthcoming initiatives or events is a great way to keep your organisation in their minds and inspire them to keep giving to your cause.

Action: Thank You Letters
First Step: Identify your top 10 donors or supporters from the last year.

Traditional: Send them personalised thank-you letters with updates on your charity's achievements, targeting 5 positive responses.
Push the Limits: Include an interactive element like a QR code that links to a personal thank-you video, aiming for 50% engagement.
Success Indicator: Responses received, engagement with the interactive elements, and repeat donations.

11. The Local Council

Local governments connect with the community in a variety of ways, including websites, newsletters, social media profiles and grant application announcements. Charities may benefit from the assistance of local authorities for marketing and other forms of support. Working together with the local council may open doors to resources and opportunities that would be difficult or impossible for charities to access on their own.

The availability of grant money for community initiatives can enable charities to host events, create flyers, posters, and other promotional materials to publicise their presence in the community. This kind of financial aid may be particularly beneficial to a charity that is operating on a shoestring budget.

Consulting with the local council when planning an event will also ensure that activities are held in accordance with existing laws and regulations. This insider information will increase the likelihood that their activities are well operated and attended, while reducing the risk of unanticipated hurdles or even fines.

However, working with local governments is not without challenges. There may be conflicts of interest or difficulty gaining assistance from local governments if the charity's goals are at odds with those of the government. Additionally, local councils may have limited resources, forcing charity organisations to compete strongly for funding and other types of help. Furthermore, the decision-making processes of local councils may be lengthy and onerous due to bureaucracy and red tape, which may impede the progress of an organisation's activities and ambitions. Furthermore, if an organisation is too reliant on the backing of its local council, it may be unable to weather changes in political leadership, budget priorities or policy.

Despite the risks involved, charities appear to benefit substantially by working with their local councils. Having the backing of a city council is very advantageous to charities spreading their message, attracting more people and raising funds. But be sure to examine the benefits and drawbacks of working with local municipalities before making any decisions.

Action: The Local Council

First Step: Identify a contact person within the local council.

Traditional: Propose regular community collaboration projects, aiming for 4 joint initiatives in a year.

Push the Limits: Pitch an annual 'Charity Day' in collaboration with the council, targeting city-wide participation.

Success Indicator: Number of joint initiatives, community feedback, and success metrics from the Charity Day.

12. Email Signatures

An often-overlooked marketing strategy, email signatures may help raise awareness about your organisation and attract new donors and volunteers. A well designed signature block can generate interest and engagement.

The subtlety and simplicity of email signatures as a marketing tool is one of their main benefits. Without resorting to explicit forms of advertising, charities may promote their causes by simply presenting vital information such as their logo, mission statement, and website link. Including a prompt such as 'Learn More' or 'Donate Now' may encourage recipients to take action and grow commitment.

It is possible to place a unique, trackable link inside the signature block to see how many people are directed to the organisation's website or particular campaign pages via the signature. With this information, a charity may better understand how their audience feels about their brand and how to improve their marketing and communication efforts.

Your email signature is a great place to promote forthcoming events, inform recipients of important news and publicise your most recent successes. You need to ensure that any information included in the signature block is explicit and well targeted to make a quick impression. The impact of the signature is diminished if recipients are unable to identify vital details or become overwhelmed by the amount of information included.

For the sake of uniformity and brand reinforcement, it is essential that all employees and volunteers use the same email signature on their communications. Achieving this may be difficult however, especially where there are a large number of employees and volunteers involved or where they are constantly coming and going.

In addition, some email applications may not properly display email signatures, or may remove photos and formatting, resulting in a less attractive or even confused appearance. In order to guarantee that the email signature looks as intended and works across all clients, contacts and devices, it must be tested on multiple platforms.

Action: Email Signatures

First Step: Draft a basic signature design with essential charity information within the next 30 minutes.

Traditional: Incorporate a call-to-action like 'Donate Now' or 'Learn More', targeting a 10% click-through rate.

Push the Limits: Rotate the signature content monthly with new achievements or campaigns, aiming for a 5% increase in direct engagement.

Success Indicator: Click-through rate, engagement with the rotated content, and direct inquiries from the signature.

13. Promotional Merchandise

Brand awareness may be boosted by distributing branded products, which will help spread the word about your organisation and its mission. Providing a visible representation of your charity's work via the sale of inexpensive items is a great way to raise awareness of your cause and strengthen connections. Merchandise sales can bring in more money to use towards attaining your goals. Pens, magnets, and keychains are all examples of low-cost promotional goods that may help communicate information about your cause.

Providing appealing products to your supporters gives them a tangible reminder of your organisation which may encourage continued support. As a talking point, merchandise can help highlight the good work you're doing. Donations increase when people have a personal connection to the cause, and well targeted promotional merchandise may facilitate that connection.

Negative aspects of promoting branded merchandise include the initial cost of investment, the resources required for storage and inventory management, and potential consequences at odds with the aims of the charity, such as the effect on the environment of production and distribution. Also bear in mind that if too many charities provide an identical product, the market will become oversaturated and sales will decline. It may also be difficult to measure the direct effect of products on your charity's marketing and overall performance.

Action: Promotional Merchandise
First Step: Identify trending or unique merchandise items.
Traditional: Offer items like custom calendars or notebooks with your charity's branding, aiming for 200 sales in three months.
Push the Limits: Collaborate with a popular brand for co-branded merchandise, targeting 1,000 sales in three months.
Success Indicator: Sales metrics, brand collaboration feedback and merchandise popularity.

14. The Leader's Network

Leveraging the personal networks of your organisation's CEO, GM or executive team may dramatically increase exposure and support.

Having your CEO or organisational leader send out a short, well-written email to their contacts is one method of tapping into their network. This should include your charity's purpose and vision statement, information about future events or fundraising efforts, and a call to action. Including useful links will make it easy for recipients to learn more about your cause and become involved. Drawing on your leader's established network in this way, your charity may rapidly increase its exposure and build trust among prospective donors.

The professional networking site *LinkedIn* provides another great opportunity for the CEO/ executive to disseminate information about your organisation. Ensure your CEO and executive staff share information about your company on their *LinkedIn* pages. In this way, not only will their contacts learn about your cause, but their followers will be able to spread the word further by sharing the material with their own audiences. To maximise your charity's connections, your leadership team should seek to team up with influential people, community leaders and volunteers.

The CEO/ leader and executive should also be active members of relevant *LinkedIn* groups where they can contribute to conversations, provide feedback on postings, and publicise the work you do. Taking the initiative in this way may help your charity gain the trust of prospective donors and establish itself as an industry leader.

Take care, though, not to rely too heavily on the CEO/leader's personal network to spread the word. Organisations must find a middle ground between using personal networks and exploring alternative promotional avenues.

Action: The Leader's Network
First Step: Identify three CEOs or organisational leaders within your network and draft a collaboration proposal.
Traditional: Host a roundtable or panel discussion, aiming to engage at least 10 CEOs/ leaders in the next quarter.
Push the Limits: Launch a 'CEO Challenge' where CEOs participate in a charity event or campaign, aiming to reach a combined audience of 500,000.
Success Indicator: Number of CEOs or leaders engaged, event attendees and audience reached.

15. A Panel of 3 Experts

One great way for a charity to make contacts and boost name recognition is to host a workshop with experts in the field. A varied and interesting experience for guests requires careful consideration of the viewpoints and areas of expertise of the specialists being brought together.

You may make the workshop more interesting and useful by having the presenters prepare cameos or case studies, or by using discussion topics to guide the discourse. This will help Inspire and motivate participants to take action.

The success of the workshop will depend on how well it is promoted. Digital marketing strategies such as social media campaigns, email newsletters and paid advertising may help spread the word about the event. Workshop buzz may be boosted and the charity's profile raised by encouraging participants to write about their experiences at the event.

Action: Panel of Experts
First Step: Identify three experts or influencers who align with your cause.
Traditional: Host a webinar or panel discussion, aiming to get 200 attendees.
Push the Limits: Organise a month-long online series with weekly sessions, targeting 1,000 cumulative attendees.
Success Indicator: Attendance count, feedback from sessions, and expert engagement metrics.

16. Social Media Content

The growing popularity of social media has impacted the techniques used by all types of charities and organisations to reach their target demographic. Charities now need to include social media marketing into their overall strategy. An organisation's audience will feel more connected and involved when they are regularly informed about events, campaigns, and other news thanks to the instant nature of social media. However the content used is all important for success. It must be developed thoughtfully and presented strategically.

Charities may efficiently and inexpensively contact millions of potential supporters and donors using social media platforms like Facebook, Twitter, TikTok, Linkedin and Instagram. In turn, charities may learn a lot about their supporters' demographics and interests via social media, which helps them refine their communications.

To develop the best content possible, you should first undertake a demographic study of your target market. By learning about their likes and dislikes, you can produce something that really connects with them. You may do this by publishing interesting pictures, making movies that people will want to share, or spotlighting inspiring true stories that connect to your cause.

Sentiment research is another crucial part of social media advertising. Using this tool, you can see how your followers are responding to your posts and learn more about what they want to see from you. Using this data, you can improve the quality of your future posts and boost the number of people who interact with and share them.

You may also utilise polls and surveys to get people involved and collect feedback on the work your charity is doing. You may learn a lot about how your followers feel about their interactions with your brand by asking them questions about their past encounters.

It is important to note that a charity cannot succeed with a marketing plan focusing solely on social media. Building and sustaining an organisation's image and credibility online requires a multifaceted approach that includes a variety of digital marketing channels. These channels include a dedicated website, targeted advertising, and electronic newsletters. Across all channels, remember that content is key.

A website is still crucial for every charity, since it establishes credibility and inspires confidence among prospective donors. If visitors can't discover a website for a charity they're interested in learning more about, they may discount the group and go elsewhere for information. A website provides a more thorough and organised overview of a charity's purpose, vision, and values than other social media channels. In addition, having a website shows dedication to the cause and the people who support it because of the time and effort invested in maintaining the site.

Connecting your website and social media accounts will boost visits to both sites. With a clickable link, interested parties may find out more about your cause and even become members or benefactors. In addition, knowing how many times a link is clicked may tell you a lot about how interested people are in your material.

Charities may expand their audience and enhance their message via advertising. Targeted advertising can attract new supporters and donors, while social media helps the charity stay connected with its present audience. When advertising and social media initiatives are combined, they promote a unified message that more effectively reaches and moves the intended audience to take action.

Charities continue to find value in e-newsletters because they allow for more direct and in-depth engagement with donors. Due to the fleeting nature of social media postings, readers may fail to notice important changes within the constant onslaught of information.With the help of e-newsletters, carefully crafted content may be sent straight to the inboxes of subscribers.The distribution of unique material, updates and achievements in this way helps the establishment and ongoing connections with supporters.

Action: Social Media Content

First Step: Review the analytics for your most popular post from the last month.

Traditional: Create a content calendar with posts 3 times a week, aiming for a consistent 10% increase in engagement.

Push the Limits: Launch a hashtag campaign or challenge, aiming to get 500 unique participations within the first month.

Success Indicator: Follower growth, post engagement rates, and participation in the hashtag campaign.

17. Free Events and Competitions

Charities may effectively connect with their communities and have a lasting influence by holding free events and seminars. These gatherings provide an excellent chance to network with like-minded individuals and leave an impact that will remain with them long after the event is over. You may build your connections with supporters, volunteers and funders by providing them with something of value, such as professional speakers, useful information or unique networking opportunities.

Finding out what people in your area care about will help ensure your workshop or event is well received. Events like charity auctions, panel discussions and educational seminars fit the bill. Easy access to the location and widespread advertising via social media, email and other means are also crucial.

When advertising, it's important to make it obvious what people should do next if they are interested, and what they will get out of attending the event. Making a landing page or registration page for an event is a fantastic method of gathering attendees' contact details and RSVPs. If you want more people to know about your event, forming partnerships with local companies and groups is a good idea.

Hosting a free event is a great way to get people interested in your cause and connected with your group without any pressure to donate. Over time, this might result in more people giving their time, money, and attention to the cause. Making an event that educates and entertains people is a great way to get people invested in your organisation's goals.

Make sure the sort of contest or competition you conduct fits well with the mission, vision, and values of your company. For example, a picture contest depicting people and their dogs is a great idea for any group that deals with the public or animals. A fitness competition is something your health group may put on. You should use your organisation's capabilities in a creative way to devise a fun and worthwhile contest.

Don't forget to think about how the competition will be hosted. Photo competitions work well on social networking sites like Instagram and Facebook, but online tools like *Kahoot* and *Quizlet* could be better suited for other types of games. You may choose which platform will best serve your contest and attract your intended audience by weighing the pros and cons of each option.

Last but not least, be sure to spread the word about your contest or competition using many methods. Spread the news by posting on social media, emailing your list, and asking your employees and volunteers to do the same. The larger your audience, the more participants you'll have in your contest.

Action: Contests and Competitions

First Step: Decide on a compelling prize or incentive for participation.

Traditional: Organise a photo contest around your charity's theme, targeting 100 submissions.

Push the Limits: Launch a community challenge with multiple levels or stages, aiming for 500 participants.

Success Indicator: Number of entries, community engagement and feedback on the contests.

18. Micro-Influencers and Ambassadors

With their unique ability to reach new audiences and spread awareness, micro-influencers have become a valuable marketing tool for organisations. These people, who have a sizable but not enormous internet following, can successfully spread the word about a charity's goals and ideals.

When compared to more established influencers with bigger followings, micro-influencers may save you money. To work with micro-influencers, you may just need to provide a free product or service in return for promotion. Micro-influencers benefit from a very responsive audience because of the high level of engagement and loyalty among their followers. If a charity wants to gain credibility and make real relationships with prospective donors, this is a great way to increase trust and authenticity within their target audience.

One way for charities to make the most of the power of micro-influencers is to launch an ambassador program. The energy and excitement of an ambassador can boost recruitment among people who are already invested in the organisation's mission. Ambassadors may be found via a number of different methods, including online communities, email campaigns and personal recommendations.

Using ambassadors to produce audience-specific material, such as blog posts or videos may help charities build stronger relationships with prospective donors and supporters. These advocates can also help spread the word by writing articles for publication on the organisation's various social media accounts.

However, it is important to find people who are a good cultural match with the charity's values and goals. A company's credibility might suffer if a partnership is not successful due to a lack of authenticity.

The time and energy needed to manage numerous micro-influencers and ambassadors is another challenge. Smaller organisations are likely to have fewer resources at their disposal, making it even more difficult for them to coordinate content production, communication and campaign implementation. Maintaining a solid rapport with the influencers and ambassadors participating in a promotion requires careful planning and organisation.

In addition, the return on investment from micro-influencer marketing may not be obvious or calculable at first. It may be difficult to assess the value of such partnerships since their results are sometimes intangible and difficult to measure in terms such as increased financial support or additional volunteer hours. When gauging the success of micro-influencer marketing methods, it's important to keep the big picture in mind and exercise patience.

Action: Micro Influencers and Ambassadors
First Step: List 5 micro-influencers who align with your cause.
Traditional: Collaborate for posts or stories, aiming for 10,000 combined engagements.
Push the Limits: Launch a month-long campaign with challenges and interactive content, targeting 100,000 combined engagements.

Success Indicator: Engagement metrics, growth in followers, and campaign-specific metrics.

19. A Local Workshop

Your charity may reach more people and provide more information about your cause by holding a local workshop that can be videotaped and made into a webinar. Workshop attendees may benefit much from a well-organised and carried-out presentation, while others who are unable to be there in person can utilise the recorded webinar as a resource.

To make a workshop presentation both instructive and interesting, it's crucial to have a detailed plan and thorough preparation. Choose a location that is easy for everyone to get to, and have all the tools and supplies you'll need on hand. Collaboration with other groups or subject matter experts may help give a broader variety of views and insights.

Creating a webinar from the recorded workshop training is a fantastic method to reach more people with your message. If you want your video and audio to be easily understood, you need to invest in high-quality equipment. The webinar may then be promoted on your website, social media and email lists after being uploaded to sites like *YouTube, Vimeo,* or *Wistia*. This will aid in spreading the word and giving individuals a helpful tool they can return to again and again as required.

Action: A Local Workshop

First Step: Identify a topic that resonates with your charity's mission and has educational value.

Traditional: Organise a quarterly workshop for the community, aiming for 50 attendees each time.

Push the Limits: Collaborate with local charities for a workshop series, targeting a cumulative 500 attendees over the series.

Success Indicator: Attendance numbers, feedback from workshops, and collaboration effectiveness.

This detailed approach can offer charities a specific, measurable, and actionable plan to elevate their marketing and outreach activities.

20. Be a Podcast / Virtual Event Guest

Podcasts have become more popular as a means of conveying news and entertainment in today's interconnected society. Marketing your charity's cause by appearing as a guest on a podcast or virtual event related to your field or purpose is a great way to spread the word about what you do and attract new supporters.

Searching for podcast appearances requires you to provide something of value to the program's audience. Think about what would make you a special guest on the program and how your audience would benefit from hearing your information or advice. Hosts of podcasts are always on the lookout for interesting people to interview, so don't be shy about contacting them with a suggestion.

After landing a guest slot, it's essential to put in the necessary time and effort to make a good impression. Create a set of talking points and key takeaways to help you convey your message and keep the discussion focused. You may gain greater self-assurance and be more prepared for the session by practising your presentation and anticipating questions the host may ask.

The opportunity to network with presenters and listeners, which might lead to future cooperation and promotion, is a major benefit of appearing as a podcast guest. Appearing on podcasts may also boost the reputation of your charity by establishing you as an authority in your sector and showcasing your work.

However, finding and pitching relevant podcasts may be time-consuming, while carrying no guarantee of success. A single virtual event or podcast appearance may have only a limited effect, so it may be necessary to make multiple appearances.

Your guest appearance should be followed up with extensive promotion across all of your organisation's communication channels to ensure maximum exposure. Promote the event through announcements on your social media pages, website and email newsletters. To generate interest in your campaign and increase participation, ask your network to listen to the episode and publicise the event.

Despite the possible downsides to being a podcast guest, the advantages may be far greater. Appearances on podcasts and virtual events may be a powerful marketing tool for charities, helping them build name recognition, credibility and lasting connections.

Action: Be a Podcast/Virtual Event Guest
First Step: List 5 podcasts relevant to your cause and reach out with a pitch by the end of the week.
Traditional: Share your charity's story and recent achievements, aiming for 2 podcast appearances in the next three months.

Push the Limits: Propose a series where various stakeholders speak across different episodes, targeting 5 podcast features in the next quarter.
Success Indicator: Number of podcast features, audience feedback, and increase in charity inquiries or support post-podcast.

21. Look Beyond Your Industry

You may learn a lot about how to improve your charity by exploring fields unrelated to your own for suggestions. Idea blogs from diverse sectors, including other charities, may provide a plethora of creative inspiration. By doing so, you will be able to learn about cutting-edge marketing strategies, methods and technologies.

If you're looking for fresh inspiration in the areas of donor and stakeholder engagement and marketing strategy development, check out blogs that cover topics like education, healthcare and sustainability. You may also get insights on the most receptive content formats used by these sectors. Drawing inspiration from other fields will increase the likelihood of attracting contributors and stakeholders to support your own cause.

Inspiration may be found in many places, and the pursuit of it can provide the drive you need to take on your own marketing initiatives.

Additionally, particularly in the realm of digital or social media marketing, staying abreast of best practice and current trends and best practices is crucial. Monitoring these blogs regularly helps keep your charity ahead of the curve and ensure its continued success.

First Step: Research and list 5 innovative marketing tactics used in other industries within the next week.
Traditional: Implement one new tactic that aligns with your charity's goals, aiming for a 15% increase in public awareness or donor engagement.
Push the Limits: Combine multiple innovative tactics for a unique campaign, targeting a 25% increase in new donor acquisition.
Success Indicator: Measurable increase in awareness, engagement, and donor acquisition metrics compared to previous campaigns.

22. Attend Conferences and Expos

At a conference or expo, you may set up a booth to promote your cause and meet new people who might be interested in donating, volunteering or partnering with you. Your booth may serve as an information hub and discussion starter, allowing you to spread the word about your organisation and the good work you're doing. Preparing materials like brochures, flyers, and charity cards to send to interested people is essential. Have a signup sheet on hand for people to join your newsletter list. Make sure you have a clear and simple message that will connect with your target audience.

Conference and exhibition participation might also take the form of giving a talk at the gathering. You can reach more people with your message and cement your reputation as an industry authority if you take the stage as a speaker. In addition to raising awareness for your cause, this may also boost your organisation's reputation and trustworthiness in the eyes of prospective contributors and collaborators.

Participating on a panel at a trade show or conference might also help your charity. Sharing the spotlight with other leaders in your sector is a great way to build professional relationships and highlight your company's commitment to teamwork. It's an opportunity to share what drives you and to lobby for the outcomes that your group cares about.

Consider the issues and themes that are most important to your organisation while looking for events to attend. You may use this to locate gatherings that share your ideals and interest your target demographic. Promote your attendance and network with other participants before, during and after the event via the use of social media and other digital channels.

First Step: Identify and register for 3 relevant conferences or expos within the next two months.
Traditional: Set up a booth and present your charity's work, aiming to network with 100+ attendees and gather 50 new contacts.
Push the Limits: Host or participate in a panel discussion or workshop at these events, targeting to influence 200+ attendees.
Success Indicator: Number of contacts made, leads generated, and follow-up actions taken post-event.

23. Reddit

Reddit is a social news website and forum, where content is curated and promoted by members through voting. When promoting your organisation on Reddit, it's crucial to see the site as a community-building tool rather than a place to broadcast sales pitches. Avoid overtly marketing your charity, but do participate in relevant discussions, ask pertinent questions and provide insightful commentary. Over time, this will increase user trust and encourage word-of-mouth recommendations, which might attract new advocates and donors.

You can reach a broad range of individuals on Reddit, since the platform has millions of members and thousands of different communities, where topics of relevance are discussed.
Building trust with users and fostering a sense of community around your organisation may be accomplished by thoughtfully taking part in conversations and offering suggestions.
Because Reddit members are usually willing to share their thoughts and experiences, you will have the potential to gain insight into your target demographic. But Reddit discussion is time-consuming, so before jumping in, think about how much of your day you are able to commit to this site.

Also be aware that direct marketing of your charitable organisation is discouraged under Reddit's rules on self-promotion. If people see your participation as merely promotional or spammy, you run the risk of facing backlash from the community, which might damage the reputation of your organisation.

Action: Reddit
First Step: Identify 3 relevant subreddits where your charity can actively participate.

Traditional: Engage by sharing stories and answering questions, aiming for 100 active engagements in a month.
Push the Limits: Host a charity-focused AMA (Ask Me Anything) targeting 1000+ interactions.
Success Indicator: Growth in subreddit engagements, feedback from the Reddit community, and AMA interaction metrics.

24. Seo (Search Engine Optimisation) Review

Search engine optimisation (SEO) is a powerful tool for raising your organisation's profile and bringing in new donors and volunteers. Performing an SEO audit, regularly updating content, and keeping tabs on your website's performance in search engine results pages can all help you identify and remedy SEO issues that are holding your charity back from reaching its full online potential, and attracting the support it needs from donors and other key stakeholders. However, it is a time-consuming process.

The correct audience may be targeted and website traffic increased by examining and upgrading your SEO keywords. Your website's visibility in search engine results for prospective donors' preferred keywords and phrases is a certain way to win over new backers.

Using keyword research tools like Google's *Keyword Planner*, Moz's *Keyword Explorer*, or *SEMrush* may help you find relevant terms. Relevant keywords, estimated search volumes, and keyword competitiveness may all be estimated with the use of these tools.

Use the keywords you've uncovered in the content, meta tags, URLs, and alt text for your images. However, you should avoid keyword stuffing to avoid being penalised by search engines.

Creating high-quality content that is useful to your audience is another strategy to boost your SEO. Articles, infographics, and videos are all acceptable forms of this content. Making your site more authoritative in the eyes of search engines is as simple as producing content that other sites will want to connect to.

Conducting frequent SEO audits to evaluate and upgrade keywords, while producing high-quality content, will positively impact your website's rankings, contributions, and support for your cause.

Action: SEO Review
First Step: Run a quick SEO audit tool for your website.

Traditional: Identify and target 5 main keywords relevant to your cause, aiming for a 20% increase in organic traffic.
Push the Limits: Create a series of articles or blogs around trending topics, targeting 3 features on Google's first page within 6 months.
Success Indicator: Growth in organic traffic, keyword rankings, and Google feature metrics.

25. Google Profile

Creating or updating your *Google* profile provides you with the opportunity to learn more about your target market. Data about your profile's viewers may be monitored and analysed with the help of services like *Google Analytics*. You can learn things like how many people visited your site, what devices they used, and where they came from by analysing this data. Using this information, you may fine-tune your marketing efforts to reach your desired demographic.

Your charity's search engine rankings may also profit from an accurate and up-to-date *Google* profile, with appropriate categories and photographs of the organisation's location and activities. An optimised profile may increase the visibility of your charity in search results for terms relating to your cause, increasing the likelihood that new contributors and supporters will come across your organisation. To ensure that your profile accurately reflects your charity's vision and aims, it must be monitored and updated on a regular basis, as must responses to reviews and social media activity.

Keeping your *Google* profile current isn't a one-and-done deal, despite the numerous advantages it provides. Instead, it takes constant care and upkeep to guarantee a positive image for your company and maximise its profile's exposure.

Action: Google Profile
First Step: Set up (or log into) your Google account and review the current information.
Traditional: Regularly update operating hours, events, and add photos from recent events, targeting a 20% increase in profile visits.
Push the Limits: Incorporate a virtual tour of a key facility or event, aiming to engage 500+ unique visitors in the next two months.
Success Indicator: Growth in profile visits, clicks to the website, and engagement metrics on the virtual tour.

26. Interactive Content and Artificial Intelligence (Ai) Chatbots

Your company can stand out from the crowd in today's competitive digital environment by using engaging, interactive content. Getting people to pay attention in this era of information overload is difficult. To differentiate your company from the competition, however, you need to provide a remarkable experience that stands out from the others.

Data and insights about your audience may be gleaned from interactive material as well. You may learn a lot about your audience's likes and dislikes by having them participate in polls or quizzes. You may use this information to make your outreach and communication more effective.

One approach to spread your message without breaking the bank is via the use of interactive material. Creating shareable, engaging content on social media, email, and other digital channels is more economical than conventional marketing methods like print and broadcast. This may let you communicate with more people for less money.

Artificial intelligence (AI) chatbots are another tool that may help charities boost participation and funding. A chatbot is a software that simulates a human-like interaction when engaging customers in a conversation. The conversational interfaces of these technologies make it simpler for customers to interact with the organisation and take action.

Chatbots are quickly becoming indispensable for charities looking to connect with their audience, share their values and simplify internal processes. These virtual assistants engage with website visitors in real-time, providing them with personalised suggestions, answers to their concerns, and help with a variety of activities by using natural language processing and machine learning algorithms. Charities may better serve their supporters, respond to their questions quickly, and improve the quality of their website's user experience by using these tools. For instance, they may point people in the direction of projects they can support financially or volunteer for. In addition, chatbots and AI bots may help charities differentiate themselves from the competition and leave a permanent mark on their audience by delivering a more collaborative and dynamic experience.

The capacity of chatbots and AI bots to automate mundane chores and lighten the strain on charity employees is a major benefit. Appointments, newsletters, contributions, and campaign updates are just some of the tasks that may be pre-set for these bots. By doing so, employees may have more time for high-value and strategic endeavours like cultivating connections with donors and brainstorming fresh approaches to fundraising.

The ability of these technologies to collect data on user behaviour and preferences is another advantage of chatbots and AI bots. Analysis of user interactions may provide useful information about visitors' interests, motivations and behaviour on a website. This information may help charities fine-tune their websites, content and marketing tactics. In addition, the data acquired by chatbots and AI bots may be used to provide users with suggestions that are specific to their interests and preferences.

Action 1: Interactive Content
First Step: Brainstorm an engaging topic or theme relevant to your charity.
Traditional: Develop quizzes or polls, targeting 500 interactions in the first month.
Push the Limits: Create an interactive story or game-based learning experience, aiming for 2,000 users in two months.
Success Indicator: Engagement metrics, user feedback, and growth in interactive content reach.
Action 2: Use a ChatBot/AI bot
First Step: Research platforms that offer ChatBots tailored for charities.

Traditional: Implement a basic ChatBot for visitor queries, targeting a 20% increase in website interaction.
Push the Limits: Develop an interactive storytelling ChatBot experience, aiming for 5000 unique interactions.
Success Indicator: User interaction rates, feedback on the ChatBot, and metrics on the storytelling experience.

Conclusion
Thank you for taking the time to read through this book on effective marketing strategies for charity organisations. I hope that you have found the information presented here to be helpful and informative. By incorporating just a few of these techniques into your marketing efforts, you can make a significant impact on your charity's journey and increase donations.

Whether it's using interactive content to tell your story or hosting a local workshop to engage with your community, every step you take towards improving your marketing strategy can bring you closer to your goals. Remember, success is a journey, and every small victory along the way is worth celebrating.

I encourage you to continue exploring new and innovative ways to connect with your supporters and grow your charity organisation. By staying open to new ideas and constantly evolving your approach, you can create a brighter future for your cause and those you serve.

Summary of Ideas

Community Radio and TV:
Partner with community radio and TV stations to create targeted programming that shares your charity's story and message, reaching a broader local audience and building awareness.

School Newsletters:
School newsletters are an effective way to reach a large and engaged audience without having to spend money on advertising.

Facebook Groups:
Creating a non-branded Facebook group is an effective and low-cost way to build relationships, create conversations, and promote awareness about your charity organisation, while rallying around the cause and creating a sense of community.

Real Time Social Media:
Real-time engagement and live video streaming on social media can be an effective way for charity organisations to connect with their supporters and attract new donors.

Promotional Kit:
Develop comprehensive promotional kits with consistent messaging to ensure brand cohesion, streamline communication, and facilitate easy access to key information about your charity.

Recruit Volunteers:
By leveraging the skills of volunteer marketing assistants, charity organisations can create a volunteer marketing team quickly, easily, and cost-effectively.

Email Newsletters:
Craft engaging email newsletters to communicate regularly with your supporters, sharing updates, success stories, and opportunities for involvement, fostering ongoing relationships and commitment to your cause.

Social Proof:
Incorporate testimonials and social proof in your charity's marketing materials to establish credibility, foster trust, and create emotional

connections with potential supporters, while maintaining authenticity and respecting privacy.

Membership Benefits:
Memberships can help market your charity by enhancing donor engagement, building loyalty, attracting new supporters, and generating recurring income, while considering the administrative burden, balancing exclusivity and inclusivity, maintaining value, and addressing competition with other organisations.

Other Local Charities, Community Groups and Businesses:
Form strategic alliances with other local charities and community groups for joint projects or events, promoting cooperation, expanding your reach, and mutually benefiting both organisations.

YouTube Videos:
Create compelling and informative videos to visually showcase your charity's mission, impact, and stories, reaching a wider audience and boosting engagement.

Handwritten Thank You Letters:
By taking the time to craft a personalised letter, you can build stronger relationships with your donors,

keep them informed about your organisation's progress, and encourage further support.

Local Council:
Collaborate with local councils to access resources, funding, and promotional channels, amplifying your charity's message and increasing visibility in the community.

Email Signatures:
Utilise email signatures as a simple yet effective marketing tool by including essential information, calls-to-action, and trackable links to raise awareness and drive traffic to your charity's website.

Promotional Merchandise:
Merchandise can help market your charity by enhancing brand visibility, fostering supporter connections, and generating revenue, while considering upfront costs, storage and inventory management, environmental impact, market saturation, and measuring impact.

Leader's Network:
Leverage the influence and credibility of your charity's CEO or leader by having them actively participate in networking, public speaking, and thought leadership opportunities to establish trust and authority in your organisation's cause.

Panel of 3 Experts:
A successful workshop can help charity organisations build relationships with other professionals in their field, make meaningful connections with potential donors and partners, and increase awareness about their cause.

Social Media Content:
Utilise social media platforms to engage with your audience, share updates, promote your cause, increasing awareness and fostering relationships with supporters.

Free Events:
Hosting free events and workshops is an excellent way for charity organisations to connect with their local communities, strengthen relationships with supporters, and raise awareness and donations for their cause.

Contests and Competitions:
Contests and competitions can be a fun and engaging way to raise awareness and funds for your charity organisation. By providing a platform for supporters to engage with your mission and compete for prizes, you can create a sense of excitement and inspire people to take action.

Micro-Influencers and Ambassadors:
Engage with micro-influencers and establish ambassador programs to tap into their niche audiences, gaining cost-effective exposure and authentic promotion for your charity organisation.

Local Workshop:
Hosting a local workshop that is recorded and turned into a webinar can be a highly effective way to increase awareness of your charity organisation and educate people about your cause.

Podcast Guest:
Leverage podcasts to reach new audiences, share your charity's story, and build relationships with hosts and listeners in your industry or cause-related field.

Look Beyond Your Industry:
Taking inspiration from different sources can help you stay fresh and innovative in your marketing efforts, making it more likely to attract donors and stakeholders to support your mission.

Attend Conferences and Expos:
Attending conferences and expos can be a valuable way to increase awareness of your charity organisation, attract new donors and volunteers,

and establish yourself as a thought leader in your industry.

Reddit:
Utilise Reddit as a community engagement tool rather than a direct promotion channel to build trust, offer valuable insights, and find potential supporters for your charity organisation.

SEO Review:
Reviewing and updating your SEO keywords is an important part of any charity marketing strategy. By optimising your website for search engines, you can attract more visitors and increase awareness about your organisation, ultimately leading to more donations and support.

Google Profile:
Creating or updating your Google Profile can offer numerous benefits for your charity organisation, including increased visibility, improved audience insights and the potential to reach more supporters and donors.

Using Interactive Content:
Using interactive content is a powerful way to engage with your audience and communicate your message in a memorable way.

ChatBots/AI:

Chatbots and AI bots can offer a wide range of benefits for charity organisations, including improved user experience, enhanced engagement, increased donations, and streamlined operations.

A FINAL NOTE TO THE READER

Thank you - the reader - for opening this book. I hope it serves you well. If it does, I'd love to know hear about your marketing efforts and impact:

www.heartsoulmarketing.com

ACKNOWLEDGEMENTS

Thank you to everyone who believed in me while I built the skills, knowledge, and experience to make a positive difference to charities and community groups, who in turn make a positive difference in the world. You've made a lasting impact. Your words, wisdom, support, or memories created together still resonate with me today.

The list includes - in order of appearance - Robyn Tymms, Lindsey and Colin Marsh, Johan Laban, Arie Cahyono, Ash Walker, Paul and Terri Marsh, Glenda Jones, Helen Powers, Helen Love, Dianne Jickell, Emilie O'Malley, Pat Burke OAM, Anna Draffin, Lynn Wood, Sarah Davies AM, Tor Roxburgh, Shawn Lee, Helen Tatchell, Cathy Bushell, Clinton Milroy, Moira Berry, Matthew Levy OAM, Kevin Newman, Lyn Watson, Hannah Brennan.

I'd also like to acknowledge the eight people I interviewed for the initial Purpose Buzz conversation series in 2023. These conversations strengthened my motivation and commitment to creating a useful resource for charities as part of my purpose. Thank you Jimmy Wales, Casey

Donovon, Ray Chamberlain, Sue Alberti AC, Tenille Gilbert, Quinton Li, Kirsty Webeck, Louise Pfeiffer.

Thanks also to an incredible group of people who gave some of their time to provide feedback and direction in the initial planning stages of this book and/or in the pre-production stage: (in no particular order): Norma Johnston, Aish Ravi, Belinda Downes, Tricia Ciampa, Brad Chilcott AM, Sarah Page, Sarah Davies AM, Caitlin Wagg, Cathy Kezelman, Sabra Brock, Mikaela Ford, Trish Kelly, Tenille Gilbert, Sue Murray, Jane Caro, Ralph Fallows, Julia Steele Scott, Jimmy Wales, Bruce Argyle, Kristin Stegley AM, Kim Downes, Narrelle Hooper, Andrew Eales, Karen Hickling, Zhi Soon, Belinda Downes, Lin Bender AM, Tim Conolan AM, Abbie Williams, Carly Ji, Dr George Taleporos, Peter Winneke, Libby Trainor Parker, Mark Zocchi, Favel Parrett.

Finally, a special mention of appreciation to Vada McDougall and Julie Taylor. Thank you for making this book possible. I hope I've done you both proud and that we meet again.

Matt Romania has spent over 15 years crafting impactful marketing strategies for charities. Starting out as a community radio volunteer, Matt has worked as a board member for grassroot community groups, freelanced as a journalist, as well as led national advertising campaigns.

Be Published

Publish through a successful publisher.
Brolga Publishing is represented through:

- National book trade distribution, including sales, marketing & distribution through Simon & Schuster.
- International book trade distribution to:
  - The United Kingdom
  - Sales representation in South East Asia
- Worldwide e-Book distribution

For details and enquiries, contact:
Brolga Publishing Pty Ltd
ABN 46 063 962 443
PO Box 452
Torquay Victoria 3228
Australia

markzocchi@brolgapublishing.com.au
(Email for a catalogue request)